MY WAY BACK

MY WAY BACK

Uncovering the Cause and Cure of Autistic Spectrum Disorder

Irving Chiang

iUniverse, Inc.
New York Lincoln Shanghai

MY WAY BACK
Uncovering the Cause and Cure of Autistic Spectrum Disorder

iUniverse books may be ordered through booksellers or by contacting:

iUniverse
2021 Pine Lake Road, Suite 100
Lincoln, NE 68512
www.iuniverse.com
1-800-Authors (1-800-288-4677)

ISBN-13: 978-0-595-38348-1
ISBN-10: 0-595-38348-3

Printed in the United States of America

Contents

Acknowledgements

I would like to thank God for providing me with the abundant experiences and many revelations that have made up this book.

Also, I would like to thank the following people:

- My belated father, James, for his love, persistence, determination and strength in trying to seek resolution of my affliction.
- My mother, Karen, and sister, Kriss, for their love and support throughout my arduous journey.
- My girlfriend, Leanne, for hanging on despite the many difficulties.
- My buddies who despite my impairment still treat me as their friends.
- Those others who have loved me and still love me for the person I am or could be.

Special mention to:

- My pastor, Hanson, and friend, Dr Wong Lok Hun, for reviewing and commenting on the draft version of this book.

Preface

This book is about my experience of an endocrinological malfunction that has resulted in much despair over the past eighteen years of my life. The initial eight years were spent without much ado. It was later during the truncated transition from adolescence to adulthood that accentuated the symptoms of the endocrinological malfunction. The past ten years have been a quest and a long journey in seeking to understand the aetiology of the disorder, searching for a cure and seeking to be understood by the general community.

The quest began without much hope but along the way, pieces of the jigsaw puzzle somehow came together and the entire picture became more obvious. The interpretations of my experience, extrapolations of research findings and most importantly the revelations from God (a.k.a. fortunate circumstances or coincidences to the non-believer) made up the many pieces of the intricate puzzle.

The purpose of this book is therefore threefold, which is as follows:

- To seek to be understood. One of the biggest fears in life is to be misunderstood. My peculiar behaviour, outbursts and underperformance made me out to be strange, portraying my character and personality in a different light. The endocrinological malfunction was in effect a barrier to my inner soul.

- To tell others of my experience and to break new ground in the current understanding of mental illnesses, including:

  a. Pervasive development disorders such as *Autism, Childhood Disintegrative Disorder and Asperger's Syndrome*;

b.   Certain adaptations of *Chronic Post Traumatic Stress Disorder*; and

c.   Personality disorders such as *Schizoid* and possibly *Schizotypal Personality Disorders*.

- To testify God's might, love, grace, mercy and truth, and to glorify his name.

At first glance, the insights given in this book may seem incredulous or even absurd, but history has shown that many great discoveries have been initially met with apprehension and rejection. It is not expected that science will initially embrace the theories postulated in this book but subsequent research, experimentation and observations will bring to light its factuality.

Would you have believed that the world was round during the 200 BC when it was geometrically proven by Eratosthenes of Cyrene in his measurement and comparison of the noon shadow at midsummer between Cyrene (now Aswan on the Nile in Egypt) and Alexandria? Or would you have continued to believe that the world is flat? Your answer would likely be the latter as most people will remain sceptical until compelling evidence shows otherwise.

This book will attempt to explain the psychological causal factors and physiological changes that have taken place that are common to the above three categories of mental illnesses. It will also explain the symptomatic differences between these three categories of mental disorders. In doing so, it will introduce revolutionary new ideas that will change the current understanding of such mental disorders.

The book will also provide a primitive cure that at this moment is effective only for a group of sufferers of these disorders, mainly of the profile of a male past puberty. It will depend on the scientific fraternity to devise variations of the physiotherapy or other surgical methods that will prove more effective and widen the scope of relieve to the sufferers of these disorders. The book will also touch on insights into how to prevent such disorders.

Parallels are also drawn between thyroid malfunction and the physiological effects of the above three categories of mental disorders. Much can be learnt from making such a comparison, as the aetiologies have much in common.

Finally, this book will serve as a medium of my thanksgiving to God. It will also attempt to explain the evidences that support the existence of a divine being that is God and Christ. These evidences are those that I have collected during my journey from non-believer to believer and from believer to disciple. I hereby dedicate this book to God and His glory. Amen.

1

Introduction

There is no current understanding of the cause of *autistic spectrum disorders* such as *autism* and *asperger's syndrome*. Some people believe that it is the result of toxins that could have been ingested at a young age. Others believe that it is a hereditary disease. This book could bring to light the cause of *autistic spectrum disorders*. While the author feels that it is unlikely that toxins are the cause of the disorder, genes do appear to influence the risk of being afflicted with the disorder.

The current understanding of the cure of the *autistic spectrum disorder* is just as obscure. While food therapies, teaching methods and antidepressants have helped alleviate some of the physical or psychological symptoms of the disorder, there is no current cure that can eradicate the problem at its root. The current therapies are only able to address the individual symptoms of the problem and not the problem in its entirety. This book will describe a form of therapy that may help in entirety a selected group of people suffering from this disorder. In future, variations of the therapy could be developed to help many others who are suffering in the same way.

There are many others who suffer the same fate of feeling isolated, disconnected and misunderstood. These people do not need to fret anymore as this book could provide them with the hope that they have long given up on; finally there could be light at the end of the long tunnel.

In my own encounters with people, I have come across many people who seem to fit the profile of having an *autistic spectrum disorder*, but have not been diagnosed as such. These people are the frequent recipients of complaints from other acquaintances about their apparent lack of sensitivities.

One example is my ex-colleague who is over fifty years old and who displays characteristics similar to that of *asperger's syndrome*. He has the tendency to interrupt during meetings and say the most inappropriate things at the most inappropriate times and that have little to do with the proceedings. He would frequently blurt out comments that are insensitive. For example, because he had somehow observed my regular toilet habits, during one meeting, he suddenly blurted out to the entire meeting that he knew that I had the habit of squatting on the toilet seat and he felt that it was really unpleasant and distasteful. At another meeting, he was complaining incessantly about a young chap whom he felt was still wet behind the years and did not have enough experience to command the high position he was holding. He did not consider that the other party who was providing the listening ear was just as young and with a similar senior position.

This same colleague also has a heightened sensitivity to light and temperature. His office air-conditioner has to be set at a particular temperature and his lighting could not be set to be too bright as well. He goes around to common areas, meeting rooms and other people's offices with his own air-conditioner controller to adjust the temperature on their air-conditioners to be just right for himself. The lighting in our offices, meeting rooms and toilets are also not spared as he loosens the fuses of the centre tubes of the three-tube fluorescent lighting arrangements to lower the luminescence levels.

The colleague also has certain interests that he particularly likes to talk about. These interests include travelling, statistics on train accidents and electronic gadgets. Whenever someone touches on these topics, he will begin a long monotone on the particular subject. The colleague also has a tendency to be pedantic. Because he is our supervisor, he frequently checks our work. When the work comes back, little change is made to the content and most of the changes made are to the grammar and spelling. In this area he is a perfectionist. He has to make sure that the grammar and spelling of the report are of the highest quality and pays little attention to its actual substance.

He also displays stubbornness when it comes to food. Whenever we have our lunches, he has to have the final say on the eating place, without due regard for other people's opinion. In the same way, if things he feels has to be carried out in a certain way is to be done differently, he would exhibit some form of petulance.

On rare occasions when we do manage to convince him to have our meals at eateries selected by us, he would without fail find something to complain about: the food, the ambience or the cost. All my other colleagues are especially reluctant when it comes to inviting him to their homes as they are mindful that their hospitality would be rewarded by his criticism.

In my youth Christian fellowship, I know of another acquaintance who seems to fit the profile of *asperger's syndrome*. He is over forty years old and is the oldest member in our fellowship. Most members are in their teens or twenties. The youth fellowship provides a comfortable place for him to fit in where he can fill up his Saturdays by following the routine of regular weekly fellowship sessions.

He is not stupid but he never seems to grow up and mature. When it comes to travelling alone, he is only able to travel on familiar routes using the public transport system. Every time a more unfamiliar route arises and even if it is described clearly to him, he refuses to travel alone on the more unfamiliar route and needs someone else to pick him up from a familiar place to bring him through the unfamiliar route. There is a seemingly lack of awareness of his surroundings and an anxiety that is associated with it.

He also has a fascination with his pet Luo Han fish. Every conversation I have with him will induce a mention of his pet fish. He will then start a monologue on a description of his pet fish and how he takes care of it.

He has an almost primal attitude towards woman or shall I say desperate. Every time a new lady comes to our fellowship, she is subject to his incessant hounding. This sometimes scares away the first-timers. He is unabashed about his attitude and still continues with it despite our open criticism. Even those girls who have been in the youth fellowship for a long time are also not spared as he constantly calls them on their mobile and tries to flirt with them in his unsuccessful way. This even includes those girls who are already attached.

He constantly harasses my pastor to set up matchmaking dates for him. My pastor has already arranged quite a number of unsuccessful meetings for him but he is still unappreciative. He reproaches my pastor for not doing enough and not working hard enough to set up dates for him. This degree of insensitiveness and unabashed behaviour does not seem to be normal.

I have another friend who used to lead a normal life. It was only when he was enlisted into the army that he started to develop a personality disorder very similar to *schizoid* or *schizotypal personality disorder*. Some people are just unable to adapt to army life. This is a period of lengthy separation from the safety of their homes and their family. It is when there is a lack of emotional support and the loss of familiarity that people are most susceptible to the enduring physiological effects of trauma. Army is a place where the "weak" are bullied by both instructors and platoon mates alike. Because instructors like to use the "weak" as scapegoats to punish the whole platoon, the "weak" are usually detested by their platoon mates. Things may go as far as what is known as the "blanket party" where the "strong" platoon mates being unhappy with the punishment dished out by their instructors, blame the "weak" for the punishment and take justice into their own hands. In the dead of night, the "strong" will cover the "weak" with blankets and beat them up.

Physical abuse alone may not be severely traumatic. It is the combination of the physical abuse and the lack of social support and emotional attachment that aggravates the result of trauma. The "weak" not only has to withstand the physical abuse, they have no one to turn to. Whereas at home, they can depend on their family members for emotional support, in the army, they have to depend on their fellow platoon mates. Yet, these same people are their victimizers.

My friend went into the army as a normal person. He came out of the army with many newborn eccentricities. He became emotionally distant, socially estranged and could not hold down a proper job. He also became easily aggressive and violent. His interests also follow a restricted pattern which includes his guitar playing, and electronic gadgets.

I feel that all their insensitiveness, social apathy, impaired awareness and restricted interests and routine seem to point towards the presence of the *autistic spectrum disorder.* All the persons mentioned in the above examples also exhibit little eye contact when communicating; slightly abnormal motor mannerisms and they seem to have difficulty forming friendships. Throughout my life experiences, I have come across many others who have similar traits that may be indicative of the *autistic spectrum disorder.* There could also be others whose simultaneous symptoms of com-morbid disorders mask the symptoms associated with the *autistic spectrum disorder.*

2

Symptoms

The main symptoms of the *autistic spectrum disorder* can be classified into twelve categories:

- Emotional apathy:

  There is an inability to understand how others feel due partly to the impairment of your senses and your feelings of not being in-sync with this world. Your emotions seem to veer towards moods of hypomania (elation) and/or depression, and you do not really feel normal emotions such as love, friendship, happiness, hope, etc.

- Hyperactivity:

  You feel that you are on the fast lane of life. There seems to be a disconnection between the speed at which your hyperactive self operates and the actual pace of life.

- Routines and habitual interests/actions:

  You follow routines and habitual interests/actions because you feel out-of-sync with life and that is the only way of making sense of life. The routines and habitual interests/actions provide an anchor to life in the presence of hyperactivity and in the absence of emotions and social reciprocity. They provide an avenue for you to relax and reduce your anxieties. Some of these interests may give a "high" similar to that of an adrenaline rush.

- Impairment of senses and hypersensitivity:

  You feel a detachment of your senses in that you feel disconnected and unable to observe and absorb most of the subtle and myriad details of what is being sensed. However, out of the many details of what is being sensed, one or two particular details seem to stand out and can sometimes be glaring and annoying.

- Verbal skills and communication

  You cannot seem to communicate well verbally because verbal communication requires immediate simultaneous responses and there is difficulty in integrating these responses. Your thoughts do not seem to be totally in-sync with the words that come out of your mouth. When you are thinking of something to say, you cannot concentrate on the words that come out of your mouth and the person's face. That partially explains why you do not use much eye contact when communicating. When you try to concentrate on looking at the person's face, you cannot concentrate on what you are saying.

  Verbal communication with another party requires hearing, thinking, speaking and seeing all at the same time and it is a difficult feat when concentration on any one of the responses results in impairment of the others.

- Anxiety

  Your anxiety is easily triggered and you feel that you have little control over your anxiety. Your anxiety is often magnified and is not commensurate with your actual thoughts of the anxious situation, which in normal circumstances would not have triggered such a symptomatic response.

- Lack of flexibility of thought

  You seem to have a one-track mind. Your thinking is rigid and you do not adapt to change or failure. Frequently, you only have one approach to solving a problem and you are not able to think of alternatives. Once you have settled on the particular approach, you are not able to vary from it even when compelling evidence that it is doomed to fail subsequently crops up. You become petulant when you are being compelled to change your approach.

- Relation and integration of experiences

  There seems to be impairment in relating and integrating your experiences with your explicit or narrative memory. Because of the failure of this integration, you are not able to form the "bigger picture" of things. As a result, you may have narrowed understanding and constricted interpretations of reality. You rely more on your implicit memory which is the memory used for learning process oriented tasks, fixed patterns and habits. Implicit memory can be likened to that of memory drawn from parallel events that are similar and repetitive in nature while explicit memory can be likened to that of memory drawn from the sequential combination and integration of different events to form a particular realisation.

- Social impairment:

  Your emotional apathy and lack of reciprocity, your disconnection from life and tendency to follow routines and habitual actions, your difficulty in relating to experiences and memory integration, the impairment of your senses and your inability to communicate effectively all come together to result in social impairment. You lack the ability to form and maintain meaningful social relationships and friendships. Social interactions are difficult because of your introverted interests, indifferent emotions and lack of empathy, lack of general awareness, anxieties, as well as impairment of your verbal communication skills.

- Learning disability and memory impairment

  Your learning is affected because of your hyperactivity and impatience, and your inability to absorb and remember diverse information. You can only absorb and retain information that is the most glaring and obvious to you. Your mind overlooks and glosses over other types of information. Your memory of facts or figures pertaining to a certain subject may be good, as these facts and figures are the most glaring and which your thoughts find particularly magnetic.

  Your lack of emotional empathy also affects your learning especially in subjects such as literature where you need to infer or draw references from your own experiences.

- Physical symptoms:

  Physical symptoms may include allergic responses such as asthma attacks, bronchial cough, eczema, etc as a result of histamine reactions. Other physical symptoms may include migraine headaches, nausea, gastro-intestinal disturbances, etc. These physical symptoms may be transient and die down as the body adapts to the permanent or semi-permanent (i.e. if there is a cure) physiological changes.

- Other symptoms:

  Depending on the personality and genetic (including race and gender) make-up of the person, there may be other symptoms. There may be poor motor coordination and abnormal gait in some persons. Symptoms such as violence and anger may also be apparent in some persons. Some autistic individuals may have a higher resilience to pain. Other individuals who are genetically inclined to suffer from depression may become depressed or manic-depressive because of their social impairment. This may also lead to the secondary effects of depersonalisation.

Other than the above symptoms, there may be other symptoms that are related to early onset of the disorder. Early onset of the disorder (e.g. infantile autism) may result in developmental delay in both language and cognition. Furthermore, it may result in mental retardation.

3

The Autistic Spectrum

There is a commonality in the physiology of pervasive development disorders such as *autism* and *asperger's syndrome* and the enduring physiological effects of *post traumatic stress disorder*. Personality disorders such as *schizoid* and *schizotypal personality disorders* may also fall in this same spectrum of disorders. Some instances of *somatoform disorder* may also be associated with this spectrum. The inability hitherto to establish this commonality is due to some of the differences between their symptoms. Furthermore their relationship may have been overlooked because only subsets of *schizotypal personality disorder, post traumatic stress disorder* and *somatoform disorder* may have associations with this spectrum.

This chapter will attempt to distil the similarities and differences in the symptoms of the various disorders, compare the similarities and on the assumption that there is a close association between these disorders, provide an explanation for the differences. For the purpose of this comparison, the Fourth Edition of the Diagnostic and Statistical Manual of Mental Disorders (DSM-IV-TR) has been largely used as the basis of reference. For simplicity in explanation, the common symptoms of these disorders have been classified as *autistic spectrum disorder* (ASD) in this book.

The form and promulgation of the symptoms depend on a variety of factors, including the age of onset of the endocrinological malfunction, the magnitude of the disorder, and the genetic and personality make-up of the person.

Autism

Autism is a disorder characterised by markedly abnormal or impaired development in social interaction and communication. *Autism* is also characterised by restricted patterns of interests, inflexible adherence to specific, non-functional routines, and stereotypical and repetitive motor mannerisms such as hand flapping, etc.

The median rate of *autism* in epidemiological studies is 5 cases per 10,000 individuals, with reported rates ranging from 2 to 20 cases. Rates of this disorder are four to five times higher in males than in females.

In the (DSM-IV-TR), the key differences between *autism* and *asperger's syndrome* are as follows:

- Qualitative impairment in verbal communication is counted as a criterion for *autism* but not for *asperger's syndrome*.

- Lack of varied, spontaneous make-believe play or social imitative play appropriate to developmental level is counted as a criterion for *autism* but not for *asperger's syndrome*.

- In most cases of *autism*, there is an associated diagnosis of *mental retardation*.

- For *autism*, there may be abnormalities in the development of cognitive skills.

- Those symptoms of *autism* that are similar to *asperger's syndrome* are also more severe and pronounced for *autism*.

There is no current understanding of the aetiology of *autism*.

By definition, the onset of *autism* is prior to age 3 years. Development of abnormalities is usually noted within the first year of life. In a minority of cases, the child may be reported to have developed normally for the first year (or even 2 years) of life.

The differences between the symptoms of *autism* and *asperger's syndrome* can thus be hypothesised to be due mainly to differences in the age of onset of

ASD. If the onset of ASD were prior to three years old, the disorder would likely be classified as *autism*. The endocrinological malfunction that occurs during early infantile development (e.g. before 3 years old), would likely lead to greater impairment in the development of the child's communication and creative thinking skills.

The endocrinological malfunction that occurs during early infantile development would also more likely lead to *mental retardation* and abnormalities in the development of cognitive skills. The younger the age of the child, the more susceptible and defenceless is the child's central nervous system towards the chemical imbalances resulting from the endocrinological malfunction. Permanent abnormalities in structure, as well as changes in synergistic properties may occur and lead to the *mental retardation* that is apparent in *autism*.

Symptoms such as the restricted patterns of interest, repetitive actions and adherence to routines are also more pronounced in *autism*. Onset of the disorder during an early age means that the child has made little sense of the purpose and order of life, and the child feeling de-linked from life, may establish non-functional and meaningless habits that provide an anchor and order to life in an attempt to reduce his anxieties.

Childhood Disintegrative Disorder

Childhood disintegrative disorder is a disorder with symptoms very similar to *autism*. The essential feature of the disorder is a marked regression in multiple areas of functioning following a period of at least 2 years of apparently normal development and the onset is prior to age 10 years. In most cases, the onset is between 3 to 4 years and may be insidious or abrupt.

There is no current understanding of the aetiology of *childhood disintegrative disorder*.

In the DSM-IV-TR, the key difference between *autism* and *childhood disintegrative disorder* is that *autism* is usually detected before 2 years of life and *childhood disintegrative disorder* usually between 3 to 4 years of life.

In the DSM-IV-TR, the key difference between *childhood disintegrative disorder* and *asperger's syndrome* is that the *childhood disintegrative disorder* is characterised by a clinically significant loss in previously acquired skills and a greater likelihood of *mental retardation*. These previously acquired skills may include language, social skills, bowel/bladder control, play or motor skills.

The onset of *childhood disintegrative disorder* can thus be hypothesised to be at the stage of childhood development between that for *autism* and *asperger's syndrome*, usually with onset between 3 to 4 years old. At this age, the child may have just learnt these skills and have not fully internalised them. Onset of the disorder at this stage of childhood development would mean a more marked regression in his functioning in these areas. *Autism* is thus characterised by onset at the stage of development when these skills have not been acquired and *asperger's syndrome* is characterised by onset at the stage of development when these skills have been fully learnt and internalised.

Asperger's Syndrome

Asperger's syndrome is a disorder with symptoms very similar to both *autism* and *childhood disintegrative disorder*. It is perhaps peculiar that they have been categorised as three different disorders in DSM-IV-TR.

The essential features of *asperger's syndrome* are as follows:

- Severe and sustained impairment in social interaction;

- The development of restricted, stereotypical and repetitive patterns of behaviour, interests, and activities; and

- The disturbance must cause clinically significant impairment in social, occupational or other important areas of functioning.

The prevalence of *asperger's syndrome* in epidemiological studies is not definitive. The male to female ratio is similar to that of *autism*.

In *asperger's syndrome*, there are no clinically significant delays or deviance in language acquisition and cognitive development. Early language and cognitive skills are within normal limits in the first 3 years of life. *Mental retardation* is also not usually observed in *asperger's disorder*.

The symptoms of *asperger's syndrome* that are commonly found in *autism* are less severe and pronounced in *asperger's syndrome*. In *autism*, restricted, repetitive and stereotypical interests and activities are often characterised by the presence of abnormal motor mannerisms, preoccupation with parts of objects, and adherence to rituals. This contrasts with *asperger's syndrome* where these are primarily observed in the one-track pursuit of a circumscribed interest to which the individual devotes inordinate amounts of time amassing information and facts.

In *autism*, typical social interaction patterns are marked by self-isolation or markedly rigid social approaches. This contrasts with *asperger's syndrome* where there may appear to be motivation for approaching others even though this is done in a highly eccentric, one-sided, verbose, and insensitive manner.

There is no current understanding of the aetiology of *asperger's syndrome*.

The onset of *asperger's syndrome* can thus be hypothesised to be at a later stage of development of the child where there is less impairment in the development of social, language and cognitive skills. Moreover the child has also understood more of the purpose and order to life and could in turn partake in restricted, repetitive and stereotypical activities that are more meaningful and functional, unlike those repeated activities in *autism* that are usually less functional or frequently non-functional.

In *asperger's syndrome*, the child's central nervous system has already developed to a considerable extent prior to the onset of the endocrinological malfunction. The central nervous system is more developed and hence less susceptible to the onslaught of chemical imbalances arising from the endocrinological malfunction. The likelihood of *mental retardation* is consequently lower.

Other Parts of Autistic Spectrum

Autism, childhood disintegrative disorder and *asperger's syndrome* can thus be hypothesised to lie on the same spectrum of disorders with the same aetiology, and with only slight disparity in the symptoms depending mostly on the age of onset of the endocrinological malfunction. This would lead one to wonder whether there is a limit to the age of onset of the endocrinological malfunction that spells the end of the spectrum. If there is no limit to the age of onset, there must be another part of the spectrum that is not currently categorised as a *pervasive development disorder* and that must have been categorised under other forms of mental disorders.

The reason why the prevalence of *asperger's syndrome* in epidemiological studies is not definitive is twofold, as follows:

- One criterion of *asperger's syndrome* is that the disturbance must cause clinically significant impairment in social, occupational or other important areas of functioning. There are many people who despite their eccentricities (having similar characteristics to that of *asperger's syndrome*) still appear to go through life without major impairment. These people may or may not be diagnosed as having *asperger's syndrome*.

- There is no clear end to the spectrum and there is no clear demarcation between *asperger's syndrome* and other mental disorders such as *schizoid* and *schizotypal personality disorders*.

Post Traumatic Stress Disorder

The essential features of *post traumatic stress disorder* are as follows:

- The person has been exposed to a traumatic event which involved actual or threatened death or serious injury, or a threat to the physical integrity of self or others;

- The person's response involved intense fear, helplessness and horror;

- The traumatic event is persistently re-experienced in one or more ways, such as having recurrent memories or dreams of the event, and/or intense psychological distress and reactivity on exposure to cues that pose a reminder of the event;

- The person tries to avoid cues that pose a reminder of the event;

- Feelings of emotional numbness and social estrangement; and

- Persistent symptoms of increased arousal such as difficulty sleeping and concentrating, and hypervigilance.

The lifetime prevalence for *post traumatic stress disorder* is approximately 8% of the adult population in the United States. Various studies have indicated a lifetime prevalence of between 1.3%[1] and 9%[2] in the general population and at least 15%[3] in psychiatric inpatients.

Traumatic exposure has been found to have an enduring physiological effect on some people. It has been found to result in lasting changes in the endocrine, autonomic and central nervous systems.[4] Other studies have delineated complex changes in the regulation of stress hormones,[5] and in the function and even the structure of specific areas of the brain. Abnormalities have been found particularly in the amygdala and the hippocampus.[6] As a comparison, *autism* has also been associated with neuro-pathological abnormalities in the hippocampus, amygdala, and cerebellum.[7]

Below is an excerpt from the book "Trauma and Recovery" that describes some of the complex and lasting effects of *post traumatic stress disorder*:

> In general, the diagnostic categories of the existing psychiatric canon are simply not designed for survivors of extreme situations and do not fit them well. The persistent anxiety, phobias, and panic of survivors are not the same as ordinary anxiety disorders. The somatic symptoms of survivors are not the same as ordinary psychosomatic disorders. Their depression is not the same as ordinary depression. And the degradation of their identity and relational life is not the same as ordinary personality disorder.

> The lack of an accurate and comprehensive diagnostic concept has serious consequences for treatment, because the connection between the patient's present symptoms and the traumatic experience is frequently lost......All too commonly, chronically traumatised people suffer in silence; but if they complain at all, their complaints are not well understood. They may collect a virtual pharmacopoeia of remedies: one for headaches, another for insomnia, another for anxiety, another for depression......

A study of people who were taken hostage also documents the long-lasting effects of a single traumatic event. All of the hostages were symptomatic in the first month after being set free, 75 percent after six months to one year, and almost half of the survivors (46 percent) still reported constrictive symptoms of emotional apathy and a sense of disconnection from life six to nine years after the event. While general anxiety symptoms tended to diminish over time, psychosomatic symptoms actually got worse.[8]

Some parallels can be drawn between *pervasive development disorders* and the lasting effects of *post traumatic stress disorder.*

Pervasive Development Disorders	Post Traumatic Stress Disorders
1. Hyperactivity and hypersensitivity	1. Hyperarousal
2. Emotional apathy	2. Emotional numbness
3. Social impairment	3. Social estrangement
4. Somatic symptoms	4. Somatic symptoms
5. Anxiety	5. Anxiety
6. Routines and habitual actions	6. Life seems meaningless
7. Learning disability and memory impairment	7. Learning and memory may be affected
8. Sometimes com-morbid with depression	8. Sometimes com-morbid with depression
9. May have aggression and self-mutilation	9. May have aggression and self-mutilation
10. Anti-depressants diminish some symptoms	10. Anti-depressants diminish some symptoms
11. May cause abnormalities in the amygdala and hippocampus, etc	11. May cause abnormalities in the amygdala and hippocampus, etc
12. Large genetic influence	12. Genes play a part

Bettleheim[9] in 1967 first postulated that *autism* is the result of trauma. When spending time imprisoned in a concentration camp, he observed many people who had effectively withdrawn from the world in order to cope with the intolerable conditions. They displayed behaviour similar to that of *autism*, being both non-communicative and exhibiting ritualistic behaviour. Bettleheim's postulations have so far been largely ignored. The rejection of his postulations could perhaps be because of fear. Society is afraid of the implications if autism is indeed caused by trauma. This could mean that adults (parents) are partially responsible for the plight of their children. Adults who abuse their children could be the key culprits for the increasing prevalence of *pervasive developmental disorders*.

Sufferers of *post traumatic stress disorder* seem to have lost their capacity to assimilate new experiences. It is…as if their personality definitely stopped at a certain point and cannot enlarge any more by the addition or assimilation of new elements.[10] Imagine an infant who stops assimilating new experiences and ceases to develop his personality at a certain point in time. We can intuitively imagine that the infant could develop the symptoms that are characteristic of *pervasive development disorders*.

After a traumatic experience, people often loose some maturational achievements and regress to earlier modes of coping with stress. In children this may show up as an inability to take care of themselves in such areas as feeding and toilet training. This is very similar to the regression in multiple areas of functioning typical of *childhood disintegrative disorder*.

Abram Kardiner[11] first introduced the notion that "traumatic neurosis" is a "physioneurosis" and that patients with *post traumatic stress disorder* remain on constant alert for environmental threat: "the subject acts as if the original traumatic situation were still in existence and engages in protective devices which failed on the original occasion…" *Pervasive development disorders* can be recognised as a "physioneurosis" where the protective device is still being engaged but the initial threat has long been forgotten. In *post traumatic stress disorder*, the physiological state of chronic hyperarousal is accompanied by difficulties in attention and concentration, as well as distortions in information processing, including narrowing of attention onto sources of potential challenge or threat. This is very similar in nature to the co-existing impairment of senses and hypersensitivity of *pervasive development disorders*. The hypersensitivity in *pervasive development disorders* appears to be a natural extension of the state of hyperarousal with the narrowing of attention onto sources of potential challenge or threat, except that the threat is long forgotten. The impairment in senses can be compared to the sense of disconnection and lack of attention and concentration felt by many survivors of *post traumatic stress disorder*.

Traumatised people loose satisfaction in matters that previously gave them a sense of satisfaction and may feel "dead to the world" After being traumatised, many people stop feeling pleasure from exploration and involvement in activities, and they feel that they just go through the motions" of everyday living.[12] Many returning soldiers speak of their difficulties with intimacy and aggression. The psychologist Josefina Card found that Vietnam veterans commonly reported difficulties getting along with their wives or girlfriends, or feeling emotionally close to anyone.[13] In the same way, sufferers of *pervasive development disorders* also feel a lack of emotional intimacy with their family and peers.

Survivors of prolonged trauma who self-mutilate consistently describe a profound dissociative state preceding the act. Depersonalisation, derealisation, and anaesthesia are accompanied by a feeling of unbearable agitation and a compulsion to attack the body. The mutilation continues until it produces a powerful feeling of calm and relief. One survivor explains: "I do it to prove I exist."[14] Similarly, autistic individuals may also self-mutilate because of their sense of disconnection from life and in an attempt to reduce their anxieties.

The similarities between *pervasive development disorders* and the enduring physiological effects of certain adaptations of *post traumatic stress disorder* support the postulation that they are of the same aetiology but on different parts of the spectrum.

The main differences between *pervasive development disorders* and *chronic post traumatic stress disorders* can thus be observed to be the apparent absence of a stressor for *pervasive development disorders*. It can be hypothesised that psychological trauma may also be the cause of *pervasive development disorders* but because of its onset at an early age of the child's development, the child would not likely remember the traumatic experience. The nature of the traumatic experience likely differs from that of the current definition of *post traumatic stress disorder* and could be in the form of prolonged separation from the parent or it could be imaginary, for example the imagined loss of his parent, etc. We do not fully understand the consciousness of a young child and he may perceive an ordinary event to be traumatic.

The effects of *post traumatic stress disorder* can be divided into the neurological effect and the endocrinological effect. The neurological effect (intrusive) induces the re-experiencing of the event and the avoidance of cues that remind the victim of the event. In more extreme cases, the neurological effect can be extended to deformation in consciousness and identity, and lead to personality disorders. The endocrinological effect (constrictive) induces the emotional numbness, social estrangement and the hyperarousal. The endocrinological malfunction will diminish but some of its residue may remain even when all the other symptoms have dissipated. This residual endocrinological malfunction could be the cause of the symptoms of *pervasive development disorders* and the enduring constrictive effects of *chronic post traumatic stress disorder*.

We can attribute the differences in the form and severity of the symptoms of *pervasive development disorders* and the enduring constrictive effects of *chronic post traumatic stress disorder* to the different ages of onset of the endocrinological malfunction and its effect on the person's psyche, physiology and personal development.

It should be noted though that not all *post traumatic stress disorders* would be accompanied by permanent endocrinological malfunction. This will depend on the age and genetic make-up of the person, as well as the nature and the person's perception of the traumatic event.

Other than constrictive symptoms that are endocrinological in nature, there can be lasting effects of trauma on the person's personality. Below is an excerpt from the book "Trauma and Recovery" highlighting some of these personality disorders:

> Three particularly troublesome diagnoses have often been applied to survivors of childhood abuse: *Somatization disorder, borderline personality disorder* and *multiple personality disorder*......These three disorders might perhaps be best understood as variants of complex *post traumatic stress disorder*, each deriving its characteristic features from one form of adaptation to the traumatic environment. The physioneurosis of post-traumatic stress disorder is the most prominent feature in *somatization disorder*, the deformation of consciousness is most prominent in *multiple personality disorder*, and the disturbance in identity and relationship is most prominent in *borderline personality disorder*......

Lawrence Kolb remarks on the "heterogeneity" of *post traumatic stress disorder*, which "is to psychiatry as syphilis was to medicine. At one time or another [this disorder] may appear to mimic every personality disorders...[15]

Dissociation appears to be the mechanism by which intense sensory and emotional experiences are disconnected from the social domain of language and memory.[16] For example, if a person enters a dissociative state at the time of the traumatic event, he may subsequently not have explicit or narrative memory of the traumatic event but only implicit memory of the event; where he may instinctually react fearfully to stimuli associated with the traumatic event but may not understand their significance.

Studies of survivors of trauma have demonstrated that people who enter a dissociative state at the time of the traumatic event are among those most likely to develop *chronic post traumatic stress disorder*.[17] It is possible that this dissociative state is induced by altercations of the endocrine system that act as a protective mechanism against the over-consolidation of the traumatic memories. Perhaps the "protective device" that Abram Kardiner mentioned was meant to protect against other adaptations of *post traumatic stress disorder*. In inducing hyperarousal and hypersensitivity, the "protective device" makes the person more alert to the "danger" at the instance of trauma. This device also acts to instil an emotional numbness that serves to downplay the emotional significance of the traumatic incident. At the same time, the "protective device" seeks to dissociate the person from memories of the event, thus lessening the impact the event has on his psyche. Where this "protective device" fails to activate or does not provide sufficient protection against the psychological onslaught of the trauma or prolonged trauma, changes in identity may form and personality disorders may develop.

Somatoform Disorders

The common feature of *somatoform disorders* is the presence of physical symptoms that suggest a general medical condition and are not fully explained by a general medical condition, by the direct effects of a substance, or by another mental disorder.

A person who has either *pervasive development disorder* or *chronic post traumatic stress disorder* but where the symptoms do not seem pronounced enough to meet the criteria for diagnosis of these two conditions, may still be suffering from the physical effects of the endocrinological malfunction, such as migraine headaches, constriction of the bronchial tubes, nausea, gastrointestinal disturbances, etc. He may come across as having a *somatoform disorder*. For example, someone who is suffering from *chronic post traumatic stress disorder* but where the stressor did not seem acute enough to have resulted in the disorder could try to make sense of his ailment through emphasis of his physical symptoms. He could be expressing his "cry for help" through exposition of his physical symptoms. Many studies have shown a close association between *somatization disorder* (type of *somatoform disorder*) and *post traumatic stress disorder*.[18, 19, 20] Somatization disorder may be induced by the dual neurological and endocrinological effects of trauma. The adjunction of the neurological deformation of consciousness with the physical effects of the endocrinological malfunction may breed this physio-neurosis.

Schizoid Personality Disorder

The essential feature of *schizoid personality disorder* is a pervasive pattern of detachment from social relationships and a restricted range of expression of emotions in interpersonal settings. This pattern begins by early adulthood.

Schizoid personality disorder is a disorder with symptoms very similar to a *pervasive development disorder*. DSM-IV-TR states that milder forms of *autism* and *asperger's syndrome* can be differentiated from *schizoid personality disorder* by more severe impairment of social interaction and stereotypical behaviours and interests.

Schizoid personality disorder is uncommon in clinical settings. Similar to *pervasive development disorders* such as *autism* and *asperger's syndrome*, *schizoid personality disorder* is more likely to occur in males. There is no current understanding of the aetiology of *schizoid personality disorder*.

If *schizoid personality disorder* is hypothesized to lie on the same spectrum as *pervasive development disorders* and *post traumatic stress disorder*, it can be postulated that the onset of most cases of *schizoid personality disorder* occur somewhere between the ages just after infantile development and prior to adulthood. It may not be recognised as *chronic post traumatic stress disorder* as the intrusive symptoms may have remained oblivious and subsequently dissipated, and the stressor may not have been recognised as significant enough to cause *post traumatic stress disorder* and contribute to the patient's emotional numbness and social estrangement.

Schizotypal Personality Disorder

The essential feature of *schizotypal personality disorder* is a pervasive pattern of social and interpersonal deficits marked by acute discomfort with, and reduced capacity for, close relationships as well as cognitive or perceptual distortions and eccentricities of behaviour. This pattern begins from early adulthood.

The prevalence of *schizotypal personality disorder* is reported to be approximately 3% of the general population. Similar to *pervasive development disorders*, *schizotypal personality disorder* is more common in males. There is no current understanding of the aetiology of *schizoid personality disorder*.

DSM-IV-TR states that milder forms of *autism* and *asperger's syndrome* can be differentiated from *schizotypal personality disorder* by more severe impairment of social interaction and stereotypical behaviours and interests. *Schizotypal personality disorder* can be differentiated from *schizoid personality disorder* by the presence of cognitive or perceptual distortions and marked eccentricity or oddness. Perhaps the over-consolidation of traumatic memories could have caused deformations in consciousness and identity apparent in *schizotypal personality disorder*.

Similar to *schizoid personality disorder*, *schizotypal personality disorder* may lie on the same spectrum as *pervasive development disorders* and *chronic post traumatic stress disorder*. If this were so, the onset of most cases of *schizotypal personality disorder* would likely occur somewhere between the ages just after infantile development and prior to adulthood. It may not be recognised as *post traumatic stress disorder* as the intrusive symptoms may remain oblivious and have dissipated, and the stressor may not have been recognised as significant enough to cause *post traumatic stress disorder* and contribute to the patient's emotional numbness and social estrangement. The cognitive or perceptual distortions could be the direct effect of the traumatic event on the person's psyche or the secondary effect of the endocrinological malfunction on the person's psyche and thought processing. Severe anxiety may also lead to schizophreniform psychosis, which may result in cognitive or perceptual distortions.

It should be noted though that some adaptations of *schizotypal personal disorder* and to a lesser extent *schizoid personality disorder* could be of an entirely different aetiology from that of the *autistic spectrum disorder* and be related instead to the *schizophrenia spectrum disorder*. These two personality disorders have been found in excess at adolescence in patients, especially men, with *schizophrenia*[21]. In one study, 5.0% of *schizoid* young people and 0.7% of controls had developed schizophrenia at a mean age of 26.5 years, as compared with an estimated population prevalence rate in the United Kingdom by 27 years of 0.31%-0.49%[22]. The similarities in symptoms of the *autistic spectrum disorder* and the pre-cursor for schizophrenia may stem from similar effects on the central nervous system caused by different aetiologies. For example, while the symptoms of the *autistic spectrum disorder* may be caused by abnormalities in serotonin synthesis, dopamine irregularities may be the main culprit for similar symptoms in the pre-cursor to *schizophrenia*.

The Autistic Spectrum

It would seem then that *pervasive development disorders* such as *autism* and *asperger's syndrome*, the enduring physiological effects of *chronic post traumatic stress disorder*, some instances of *somatoform disorder* and some adaptations of personality disorders such as *schizoid* and *schizotypal personality disorders* may all lie on the same spectrum of disorders. While it is evident that *autism* and *asperger's syndrome* are more predominantly found in males, both *schizoid* and *schizotypal personality disorders* also seem to be more predominant in males. In a later chapter, we will discuss the possible reasons for the gender differences.

Clear genetic links have been established between *autism, asperger's syndrome* and *schizoid personality disorder*. *Autism* and *asperger's syndrome* have been found more often in members of the same families.[23] Studies have also found that significantly more parents of autistic children have mild *schizoid personality* traits.[24]

Nagy & Szatmari[25] initially described 20 children as *schizotypal* and after recognising their similarity with *asperger's syndrome*, dropped "*schizotypal*" in favour of "*asperger's syndrome*".

Evidence from various studies also now suggests that it is possible that autism is one part of a broader phenotype of social-communicative difficulties[26]. The *broader phenotype autism* is conceptually similar to *autism* and *asperger's syndrome* but the traits and behaviours are less severe and usually do not come to clinical attention. The prevalence of *broader phenotype autism* is estimated at around 4%[27] of the population.

The diagram below depicts the probability of *mental retardation* versus the age of onset of the endocrinological malfunction:

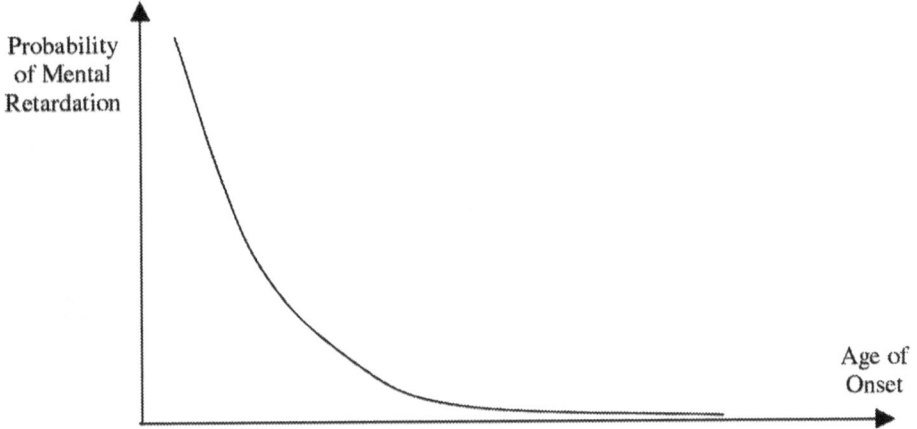

The Autistic Spectrum

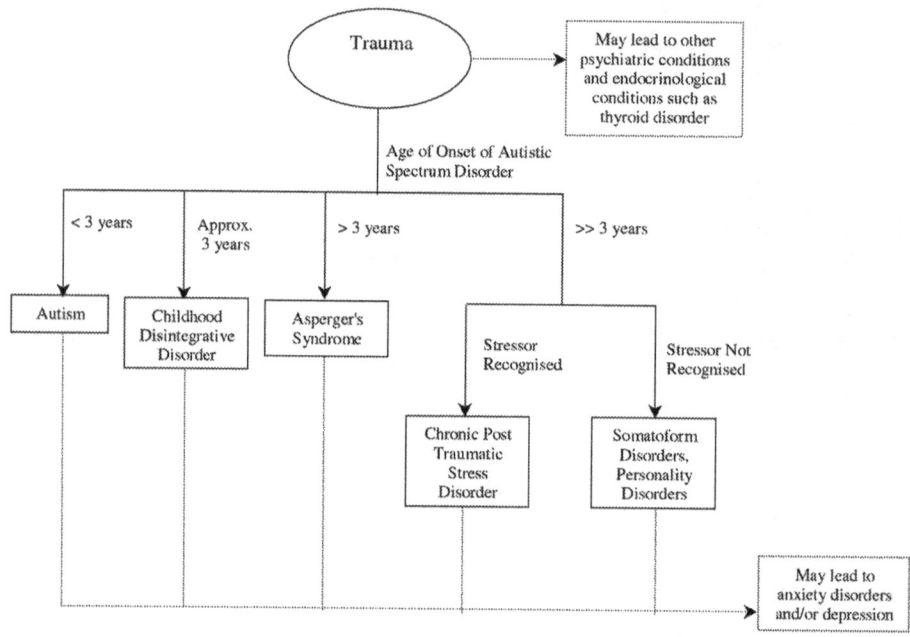

Important Points to Remember

- *Autism, asperger's syndrome* and *childhood disintegrative disorder* may lie on the same spectrum of disorders.

- The enduring physiological effects of *chronic post traumatic stress disorder* may lie on this same spectrum.

- Some adaptations of *schizoid* and *schizotypal personality disorders* may also lie on this same spectrum.

- Some instances of *somatoform disorders* may be related to this spectrum.

- Even though these mental illnesses lie on the same spectrum (*autistic spectrum disorder*), they are classified differently due to the different ages of onset of the disorders, and the presence or absence of explicit "stressors".

- *Mental retardation* is more likely to occur at early onset of the disorder.

- The *autistic spectrum disorder* is caused by an endocrinological malfunction.

- The endocrinological malfunction is the permanent residual effect of the endocrinological response to the trauma.

- The endocrinological response may act as a protective mechanism against the over-consolidation of traumatic memories and its adverse effects on the person's psyche.

- Failure of this protective mechanism may result in the deformation of consciousness and identity.

4

My Life Story

Horror Drama

There is one horror drama that left a deep impression on my mind. The name of the movie is "V" which is the acronym for "Visitors". These visitors were aliens who under the guise of humans, infiltrated the human race. Their objective was simple and it was to destroy us. Most of these aliens were evil except for the renegade few who had some compassion for the human race and secretly helped us. These aliens had a fake human skin that they donned on to near perfection. It was almost impossible to distinguish aliens from humans.

I watched this drama serial when I was around ten years old. It introduced into my subconscious the possibility that humans may not appear as they seem. There may actually be more than meets the eye. It left a deep impression on my mind because its induction into my subconscious subsequently led to a nightmare episode that was to have severe and long-lasting repercussions.

Nightmare Episode

The nightmare happened when I was around ten to eleven years old. The exact year I cannot recall. I remember the dream vaguely. It was not only about fear, but also about separation. An abrupt fear by itself will probably not lead to psychological and physiological imbalances. After all, who has not seen a thriller about serial killers or movie about poltergeists that employ shock tactics to intensify the adrenaline secretion in our endocrine system? Likewise who has not woken up from a nightmare episode breaking out in cold sweat?

There have however been extreme cases of fear or shock that have lead to psychological and endocrinological imbalances. The current medical nomenclature for this type of mental disorder is *post traumatic stress disorder.* In such cases, either the person's physical integrity has been threatened, the person has had first hand experience of the mutilation of another person, or the person's experience of fear or shock has been coupled with some form of separation from a loved one. For example watching your close buddy die in war, or learning of your loved one's death in an accident can lead to *post traumatic stress disorder.*

In the dream there was only my family and me. Slowly and surely, one by one, they transformed into poltergeists. In which order I could not remember but it started off with the realisation that one family member had become an entity quite beyond my understanding: a stranger and a being that I perceived as malevolent. As this happened, the instinctive reaction was to seek consolation and protection from another family member. However, it came to dawn on me that the other family member had also become a transcendental evil quite beyond my recognition. This cycle continued until I came to the full realisation that my mother, father and sister had all been epidemically infected and had undergone the eerie transformation. The fear and shock magnified exponentially as each realisation set in. At the end of it all, I had gone beyond the "edge" and past my "breaking point". I was alone with nobody to depend on. I had to also pretend to have transformed and assimilated for fear of the consequences if I was to be found out. After that, I remember waking up in tears: shocked, full of despair and disoriented.

I surmise that at that moment, a psychological and physiological change had taken place. The physiological change was to cause the immediate onset of symptomatic side effects and in later years to come, a lot of despair as I struggled to comprehend and rationalise my peculiarities in the transition from adolescence to adulthood.

Asthmatic Attack

The following night, as I was going to sleep, I had a strange feeling in my lungs and there was this perception by me of having difficulty breathing. I was not gasping for air but somehow the use of the intake of air did not seem efficient. At that point, I thought I was going to die. As there were no outward signs of any difficulty breathing and I did not have any history of asthma, my parents told me that it could be just my imagination and they would send me to hospital only if it worsened. I coaxed myself that there was nothing wrong and tried to get back to sleep. After some time and with some difficulty, I finally managed to fall asleep.

The next day, there was no recurrence of this phenomenon. This was a one-off experience and although at that point I could not understand the factors of causation, the experience left an indelible mark in my memory, which was not to be erased in spite of the upheavals and anarchy that my psyche was subsequently subjected to.

In reality, this experience was really not that exceptional and can be explained by the sudden increase in serotonin that led to the constriction of the bronchial tubes and the "asthmatic" attack that followed. The subsequent non-recurrence of the phenomenon can only be explained by the natural adaptation of the body to the increase in serotonin.

Hyperarousal

Although the nightmare episode was an imagined episode and not real, it resulted in a sustained period of hyperarousal. I became hyper-vigilant and reacted fearfully to every dark shadow and noise that could be indicative of a malevolent being. Prior to the nightmare episode, I had no difficulties sleeping alone. Subsequent to it, I developed an intense fear of the dark. I could not fall asleep unless I had my mother beside me to coax me while I fell asleep.

The fear and hyper-vigilance was not only pervasive during the night when it was dark, it was also apparent during the day when I was alone. I felt frightened when I was alone at home during the day. I would wait anxiously at the balcony for any of my family members to return home. I would then furtively look through the "peep hole" of our main door with expectancy of their return. Even this was carried out with much fear as I was uncertain of what I would find on the other side of the door.

Answering natures call was also a problem as I would feel frightened using the toilet alone. If it was just to relieve my bladder, I would rush through it. If it required a longer time, say to clear my bowels, I would plead with one of my family members to stand on the other side of the toilet door and talk to me while I was doing my business.

I remember one particular day when I missed my school bus and I had to take the public bus from school to my home. Usually the school bus would fetch me right to the doorsteps of my home. If I took the public bus, I had to get off at the bus stop, which was quite some distance away, and from there, make my way through a housing lane. The lane was shaded by many trees and at that time, I perceived it to be dark and pretty deserted. This was not really true, as there were rows of houses on both sides of the lane and there were people in them but who were not clearly visible to me. I distinctly remember the fear as I made my way through the housing lane. I was clearly reactive to every slight sound and movement. Even the rustling of the leaves in the wind provoked a reactive fear in me. It took an immense effort for me to traverse through the short lane. I really dreaded the feeling and from then on, I was extremely cautious to make sure that I was always on time to take the school bus home.

I do not recall exactly how long the period of hyperarousal persisted, but from my faint recollection it seemed to last for less than a year. Even though hyperarousal is a classic symptom of *post traumatic stress disorder*, I was never diagnosed with the disorder as the traumatic event did not occur as part of reality and it did not seem significant enough to elicit such a pathological response.

Although the hyperarousal dissipated, it left behind a residual hyperactivity and hypersensitivity. Even though I had cognitively overcome the fears related to the trauma, the body was already fashioned to be constantly hyper-vigilant and alert to particular forms of external stimuli. This alertness came through as hypersensitivity in the backdrop of hyperactivity. The traumatic memories had become insignificant but the induction of the trauma had elicited an endocrinological response that had become permanent.

Regression

Following the nightmare episode, there was an increased frequency of the need to use the toilet to relieve my bladder. This was particularly troublesome when I did not have easy access to the toilet. Long journeys proved bothersome as I frequently had to stop to use the toilet. This was sometimes at the expense of others especially when I was on group tours. While watching movies in the cinema, I was also frequently interrupted by my visits to the toilet.

On one occasion when I was on my way to my grandparents' home, I was feeling urgent and found that I had to concentrate very hard to make sure that my urinary tract did not give way suddenly. Throughout the whole journey, I was focusing on my bladder control and was somewhat successful. As I approached the doorway of my grandparent's home, I subconsciously knew that I was nearing my destination and inadvertently relaxed myself and lost focus of my bladder control. It was at this moment that it gave way. My clothing was drenched with the yellowish and pungent liquid. I felt utterly mortified. Even though the loss of my bladder control in a public arena was a one-off experience, it occurred when I was already aged ten and not long after the nightmare episode. I felt totally embarrassed and took special care to visit the toilet as and when I had the chance even when I did not have an urge to.

The deterioration of bladder control was also apparent during my sleep. I remember wetting my bed on a few occasions during this period. There was one occasion when I had a dream and in the dream I was visiting the toilet. Standing in front of the urinal, I let loose. My dream was interrupted by the feeling of wet trickles along my pelvis and thighs. My mother had to wash the bed sheets and bring the mattress out onto the balcony to dry in the sun.

Both *childhood disintegrative disorder* and *post traumatic stress disorder* have been associated with the loss of previously acquired skills, including the loss of bowel and bladder control. In my case, I had a momentarily lapse in my bladder control skills and had to quickly re-acquire them.

Eczema

In the months following the incident, eczema settled into my fingers and toes like wild mushrooms growing in the garden. Clinicians initially wrongly diagnosed it as fungal infection that could have been caused by regular swimming in the condominium swimming pool. They subsequently diagnosed it as eczema, which on hindsight I realize with some certainty is the correct diagnosis.

The onset of eczema can be explained by the sudden increase in serotonin, which led to histamine reactions.

The eczema subsequently disappeared without any reason. I surmised that my body had adjusted to the permanent increase in serotonin and in so doing modulated the histamine reactions.

Gastro-intestinal disturbances

The period after the nightmare episode was accompanied by gastric pains that were inexplicable. I could be walking along the corridor outside my classrooms and suddenly feel intolerable gastric pains that seemed to me like a knife piercing through me. When the gastric pains came, my intuitive reaction was to squat down. Squatting down did alleviate some of the pain but only modestly. I tried visiting the washroom but it was to no avail. Going to the potty did not seem to lessen the pain. I was powerless in preventing or diminishing its effects. I just had to wait patiently while the pain dissipated on its own.

Other Physical Symptoms

Up to then and so far as my cognitive awareness could allow me to recall, I did not previously have the symptomatic complaints that were to follow the incident. In the months that followed the incident, other physical symptoms including migraine, nausea, and bronchial cough set in spontaneously. I remember a period of time when I frequently woke up in the morning with migraine. Clinicians explained that it was probably just tension headaches and brushed it aside. I recall wondering why the migraine still occurred even though I did not feel particularly tense nor was there anything I had cause to be worried about. Simple actions like brushing my teeth or entering a toilet that was obnoxious to my senses would lead to nausea. For me, this was an entirely new experience. The development of a bronchial cough also began during this same period. This can be vividly described by one incident when I could hardly contain an incessant cough that ensued after consuming a packet of raisins. All of the above symptoms have been clinically linked to increased serotonin. Similar to eczema, these symptoms were short-lived and disappeared subsequently. At that point in time though, these symptoms seemed inexplicable.

Another symptom that was apparent during that time was that there was a pain between my groin and anus that was triggered off by the impact that was made by my jumping from high places. As I had never felt this before, it could be of some significance. However, I have yet to attribute any reason for this pain but perhaps it could have some relation to the onset of the endocrinological malfunction.

Hyperactivity

Increased hyperactivity was also apparent. Two incidents that happened not long after the nightmare episode appear to demonstrate this point. The first incident was of me doing my entire homework in red ink, which was not customary of my obedient and obliging character. Being infused with the increased hyperactivity, I remember thinking that I wanted to try out something different from the norm. All the while up to that point in time, I had always been doing my homework dutifully in the conventional blue ink and there was no reason for any change. The only reason for change was a change in my mood and to a lesser extent, my perception and mentality.

The second incident was of me surreptitiously emptying an entire bucket of water over my tenth-floor residential balcony without any rhyme or reason. I can only assume that I was inspired by the increased hyperactivity. This spurred my ninth-floor neighbour to climb up a flight of stairs to complain of a crime, of which I denied fervently.

As of now, I can only recall these two incidents. I am however pretty certain that these two incidents were not isolated and there were many more instances of me succumbing to the increased hyperactivity and acting foolishly. Although these two incidents are seemingly minor in pathological terms, they were totally out of my character and pointed to a sudden and abrupt psychological and physiological change.

The increased hyperactivity did not disappear like the other physical symptoms. The increased hyperactivity prolonged throughout adolescence and persisted in some form despite the subsequent onset of depression.

A constant feature of the hyperactivity was that I could not sit or stand still for a long time. My mom used to comment that I had a conical shaped bottom as

I could not sit still for long. I also found it difficult to think while I sat or stood up. Studying was done lying on my bed or on the floor, pacing around the house, or simultaneously while carrying out other activities: taking a crap, eating dinner, watching TV, or having a shower.

As I grew older, I developed a habit of walking long distances to think. It was while walking that my thoughts were most coherent. It was during these times of deep deliberation that I gained significant insights into my problem.

Impairment of Senses and Hypersensitivity

The endocrinological malfunction also affected my senses and consequently awareness. In particular, it seemed to affect sight and the mental adsorption of images. It seemed to affect all my senses but its effect was more obvious on sight perhaps because visual images are more complex and subject to nuances. Not saying that the other senses are not subject to nuances but just that the other senses usually do not have to be particularly sensitive to myriad nuances for everyday use. For example, taste does not have to be particularly sensitive to many complex details to be able to function properly unless the person is a food critic or wine connoisseur. In the same way, hearing may not have to be particularly sensitive to a whole range of sounds to be able to make out what someone else is saying but may have to be so to be able to tune a guitar without a tuner.

The endocrinological malfunction seemed to frequently bring about my attention to a particular aspect of what is being sensed, with increased focus and sensitivity towards that particular aspect that stands out and the trade-off is less emphasis on other aspects of what is being sensed. Hence, I frequently observed only a particular detail of what is being sensed but was unable to observe the other simultaneous details and unable to capture what is being sensed as an entire picture. Frequently when nothing particularly stands out, the effect is that what is being sensed becomes totally vague and indistinct. For example, in a visual sense, I may seem to be looking at something but was not really seeing it.

One result of this disability as I grew older was that I could not seem to get a clean shave. I had an incomplete view of my face and very often, I would leave patches of my facial hair unshaved. In the same way, I fared poorly in those tasks that required a full and complete view of the task-at-hand.

Another task that I could not master was that of taking photographs. Taking photographs requires the viewing of both the person in the frame and the background images. If I tried to focus on the background images to make sure that all the pertinent images were captured, I could not focus on the person whose photograph was being taken. If I tried to focus on the person, the camera lenses may not capture the pertinent background images. Often the photographs that I took either had parts of the person missing or parts of the pertinent background images being missed. Even if I managed to capture the person and background images in the same frame, the relative proportions of the objects in the photograph were usually inadequate.

Let's say that there are five objects in the kitchen: there is a table; on the tabletop there are some cups; behind the table there is a refrigerator, an oven and a sink. If I am looking across at the kitchen from afar, all these items should be within the range of my vision and I should be aware of most of these objects. The impairment of senses and hypersensitivity allows me to only look at one particular object at one time. I may be only looking at the table and not noticing the other objects. The hypersensitivity to one particular object results in impairment in your senses to the other objects.

Another aspect of this problem was the difficulty in judging distances. Visually, images may appear more two-dimensional than three-dimensional. This results in a lack of spatial awareness. When a computer portrays a 3-D image, it requires substantially more memory. Portrayal of digital 3-D images requires the integration of many 2-D images as seen from different angles. The quality of the 3-D image would depend on the number of 2-D images being integrated. In the same way, hypersensitivity highlights the most obvious 2-D image and lessens the impact of the other 2-D images. The effect is that visual images would appear more 2-D than 3-D.

This may also explain why people with *autism* or *asperger's syndrome* are more object oriented in their visualisations and less able to recognise faces. Recognition of objects usually requires emphasis on fewer and less complex details, whereas recognition of faces requires simultaneous emphasis on various myriad aspects of the person's face. It is because of the inability to capture all the myriad aspects of the person's face as a complete picture that it leads to difficulty in facial recognition. The autistic person may only be able to capture one aspect of the person's face at any one time.

I would liken its effect on sight to trying to look out at a painting in the train station from a speeding train. On the speeding train, you can roughly make out what the painting in the train station is about and you will also be able to pick out the particular aspect of the painting that is most obvious. However you would not be able to study and enjoy its finer distinctions. Likewise when a person is infused with increased serotonin, his mind becomes hyperactive and works just like the speeding train. His cognition is affected and he becomes more aware of only the most obvious aspect of his surroundings and less aware of his general surroundings.

I am suffering from mild myopia, ranging from around one hundred to two hundred degrees in both eyes. Despite this disability, I have an aversion for wearing spectacles. Wearing spectacles seem to accentuate those images that I am hypersensitive to. When I wear my spectacles, I am forced to focus on these images and this makes my eyes and my mind feel overworked. When I attended lessons in school, even if I am not able to see the board, I would refuse to put on my glasses. I would either ignore what was being written on the board or if it was something important, I would squint and try to make out the vague figures. When I could not see these figures even by squinting, I would just ask other people what was being written or read from their notes.

It seems strange to me then that some people with *asperger's syndrome* have a predominantly visual style of thinking, when considering the disabilities to their visual senses. On a personal note, my experience was that the disability in my visual senses was extended to my mental visualisation of images and as a result the images conceived in my mind were always blurred and indistinct.

The visual disability may also explain why there is a marked decrease in eye contact and a reduction in the use of multiple nonverbal behaviours such as facial expression, body postures and gestures to regulate social interaction. Eye contact comes naturally when a person is able to assimilate the face of the person he is communicating with. It becomes really unnatural when you cannot seem to "see" the person you are talking to. Nonverbal behaviours such as facial expression, body postures and gestures are learned behaviours through observation of other people and how they communicate. Being less visually aware of how other people communicate would affect the ability to pick up such habits. Also, with the partial impairment of sight and the adsorption of visual images, there may be less emphasis on the use of visual communication.

Several autobiographies of people with *asperger's syndrome* have included references to problems with focusing on one person's voice when several people are talking, or a distorted perception of speech. Parallels can be drawn between this auditory disability and the visual disability. Both seem to point towards a disability in sensing when there is a complex array of stimuli at a particular time.

It is noted also that my written expression is a lot better than my verbal expression. This could be because when I talk to another person, I have to listen to the other party, think about what I want to say, maintain eye contact, and be aware of my surroundings all at the same time. Verbal communication requires an integration of visual and auditory senses with the process of thinking. It is the impairment of such integration in an autistic person that results in impairment of verbal communication. On the other hand, writing does not require such considerations as what is being written can be slowly crafted in a relaxed environment where the use of visual and auditory senses are minimised and full concentration can be placed on the thought processing.

Because of the increased emphasis on particular aspects of what is being sensed, the autistic person becomes hypersensitive to these aspects. For example, an autistic person may be particularly sensitive to being touched, bright light, unpleasant sounds and/or repulsive smells. The added emphasis on these particular aspects makes them all the more glaring and often intolerable. It seems as if the increased serotonin has disabled cognition and amplified the person's instinctive responses. In effect, the person has become more of an "animal" and less of a "man".

On a personal note, I had an increased distaste towards unpleasant odours which frequently made me feel nauseous. I also had a dislike for being touched, usually finding it ticklish and feeling squeamish as a result. This was apparent upon the onset of the endocrinological malfunction. I started to resist being hugged by my mother. She thought it was a phase of me growing up.

I also steadfastly refused to wear any accessories. I do not wear wristwatches and during a time when hand phones were uncommon, I had to rely on other people's watches to tell the time. I would peer over people's shoulders to peep at their watches, often eliciting a suspicious look from them.

After I got attached to my girlfriend, she insisted that I wear one half of a pair of matching rings as a symbol of our love and commitment. During the initial period and despite the discomfort, I reluctantly wore the ring but only when I was out with her. I wore the ring in obedience to what I initially perceived as an obligation necessary in a relation. I could not at that time conceive that there could be flexibility in a relationship and that I did not necessarily have to give in to her demands. I just had to explain clearly to her of my discomfort but my rigid way of thinking prevented me from emphasizing my point.

Another feature of hypersensitivity to touch was my dislike for many types of clothes. My preference for clothes was restricted to only those that were very smooth on the touch, loose and with no constriction at the neck and arms. Ties were particularly abhorred as I felt terribly suffocated by them. The worst were those shirts that were very tight at the armpit and which I felt tickled by.

Hypersensitivity to sound was not that obvious. Nevertheless I have noticed that when I went to discotheques and stood near the amplifiers, I had to cup my hands over my ears to muffle the glaring noise. Those people near me who were exposed to the same decibels did not react in the same way and continued rejoicing in the music. I have often wondered why that was so. On the other hand, there was also impairment in my hearing especially when there are many diverse and coincident sounds. Many of my friends and family members have often complained that I do not pick up my calls when they ring me on the mobile. It is not that I choose to ignore them. It was just that even when I set the volume of the ringing tone to maximum, I was not able to hear the ringing of my own phone. I could hear the phone ring when there was little ambient noise, but when it came to public places, the hustle and bustle of the background easily drained out the ringing of my phone.

Listening to music was also superficial as I could only make out the melody but could not distinguish the lyrics of the song. Even the discernment of the melody was shallow as I did not notice the assortment of the instrumentals. I could only catch the general melody, but paid no heed to the lyrics and the instruments.

The impairment of my senses was not restricted to my five senses but also extended to my spiritual sense. I think God may have had some difficulty communicating with me. While other people could sense the presence of the Holy Spirit, I could only feel It subtly. It was only when the presence of the Holy Spirit was overwhelming that I could sense It. Sometimes I felt a little joy; other times I felt a bit of warmth; at times I felt peace and calm.

I have seen people who are very certain when God communicates to them through different means. They act on God's will with confidence. With my poor receptiveness, I am always uncertain when God communicates to me. I usually have to validate that God has communicated to me by calculating the probabilities of such and such coincident events occurring. Where the probabilities are low, I would surmise that the events could not likely have been coincidental and are probably God's sign that He wants me to do something.

There was also a reduced sensitivity to pain. There was an incident when I fell down and bruised my knees badly. I remember staring at myself in the mirror and wondering why my response to being bruised was so different from how it was previously. I felt numbness, both emotionally and physically. Why was it that I did not really feel the pain and any emotion? My recollections of my previous responses to such injuries were those of pain and misery. Yet this time round, I felt only numbness. It seemed almost unreal......

Isolation and Elation

Prior to the episode of the nightmare, I made friends easily and had many friends. These friends included schoolmates, neighbours, cousins and children of my parents' close associates. Making friends was through shared interests and through social and emotional empathy and reciprocity.

With the increase in serotonin and the onset of the hyperactivity, my friends and I started to distance. There were no longer shared interests as I was now preoccupied with a few stereotypical and restricted patterns of interest that were abnormal in intensity. In this case, I was specifically preoccupied with video games and martial arts serials and at that time and for a few years hence, these were my only real interests. Although I did subsequently pick up other interests such as classical science-fiction novels and basketball, the pattern was still the same as I was completely absorbed in these interests. Nothing else interested me and nothing else in life meant anything to me. These interests had an addictive effect, as they stimulated and transformed the hyperactivity into some form of elation. The "high" came with victory, which was the quintessential element of my restricted interests. From video games, I felt the "high" of defeating the enemy. From martial arts serials, I felt the "high" of the protagonists defeating his exponents. In the science-fiction novels, I felt the high of the hero defeating his enemy. In basketball, I felt the "high" of defeating my opponents.

Even though I relished playing basketball, I never really excelled in it. I was best at rebounding because it was just me and the ball. With the natural spring in my steps and my quickest reaction to the ball coming off the boards, I managed to grab most of the rebounds. There was an associated hypersensitivity to the ball that resulted in me reacting fastest to it. My aptitude at rebounding was however at the expense of my general awareness. While I was hypersensitive to the ball, I was not really aware of the other players and the position of the hoop. This was not helpful in my general game.

When it came to computer games, I excelled in games that were static and that required planning and strategies. For example, as the army general in one game, I had to control my funds, rations and recruitment. I did particularly well as I managed to significantly expand my territory. On the other hand, I fared poorly in games that were dynamic and required a general awareness and psychomotor skills. For example, in games that involved one to one combat with an opponent, it was necessary to have an awareness of the complete situation and a quick response to any movements by your opponent. The punches and kicks came in fast and furious and I was hardly aware of them enough to elicit a response. No matter how much I practised, I could never master such games.

Outside of these interests, my life was routine and had no meaning. Life only has real meaning when one can feel emotions. I was now like a stoic robot being previously taught and now obliged to carry out my daily specific routines. I was now emotionally distanced from people and my environment. I did not empathise with people. I did not in the normal sense feel love, sadness or compassion. The only distinguishable emotion I felt was elation. Was that a state of nirvana?

Learning Disability and Memory Impairment

With the increased hyperactivity, I did not particularly relish doing my homework or studying for examinations. In primary school after the onset of the increased serotonin, work was still relatively simple and I could manage pretty well. My intelligence could still offset my newfound disabilities. In secondary school, because of the huge workload and the large amount and variety of diverse information that had to be understood and committed to memory, I initially did not do well. There was a decreased adsorption, comprehension and retention of mass information that was to be acquired, analysed and remembered through classroom lessons and self-study.

In lower secondary I scored well in mathematical subjects but badly in humanities. The reason being that intelligence was sufficient to master mathematics. For mathematical subjects, once the underlying principles are understood one can score pretty well. This can compare with autistic children who have exceptional abilities, having mastered the principles underlying their abilities. In contrast, humanities require a mixture of intelligence, empathy, patience and information retention, which were all vital. Of this mix, I only had intelligence. The increased hyperactivity was a thorn in cultivating any patience. It has also been observed clinically that increase in serotonin impairs learning and memory, both of which are vital for the respective adsorption and retention of mass amount of information, which is essential for the mastering of any humanities subject. Although some autistic individuals have been observed to have gargantuan memory when it comes to remembering facts and figures related to a certain topic, this memory is selective and only restricted to a specific topic. When it comes to diverse information of various subjects, the autistic individual has difficulty recollecting information on most other areas that do not appeal innately to their psyche. Impairment in emotional empathy also meant a poorer grasp of humanities such as literature and history, which are a lot about human relations.

Going into higher secondary, I modified my method of learning humanities to overcome my disabilities. Instead of trying to absorb and understand what I was learning, I began to place more emphasis on "rote" learning. I started to memorise text systematically without any real understanding. This was highly effective for examinations but was not beneficial for my general knowledge and intellectual maturity. Its effect was short-term memory of the subject sufficient for recitation during examinations.

Another point to note was that during higher secondary, slight depression had started to set in. The depression had to do with a friend of mine who had previously persistently involved me in his interests and had become a permanent fixture in my life. It was during higher secondary that he started to ignore me and became aloof. As I did not understand why that had happened or what I had done wrongly, I grew slightly depressed. The depression had some effect in reducing hyperactivity and perhaps in increasing my introspection and rationalisation of the world and human behaviour, it allowed some form of distant emotional empathy more as an observer rather than a participant.

To overcome the hyperactivity in the course of studying, I resorted to mini-breaks after every half-hour or so of study. I also resorted to moving around all over my home looking for different niches and different postures to study in. I sometimes paced incessantly while studying, having made countless rounds (up to one hundred rounds per cycle) around my dining table. Other times I would watch television or shower while studying. In a way, I was a slave to hyperactivity.

Libido

The onset of the endocrinological malfunction occurred towards the inception of puberty. That was a time when I started to take notice of girls. While I had already discovered the sense of physical pleasure associated with physical contact of the genitals, masturbation was carried out rarely and only when the visual and imaginative stimuli were intrusive. One of the side effects of the increased serotonin was the increased libido and urge for masturbation. Upon the onset of the increased serotonin, masturbation became a frequent ritual even without the presence of any stimuli. I had become dependent on it to reduce the stress and the hyperactivity associated with the increased serotonin in my body.

While hypervigilance usually results in hypersensitivity to stimuli that would warn of impending danger, the lack of any realistic danger resulted in the "objects of danger" being shifted to other forms of stimuli. One of the external stimuli that replaced the "objects of danger" was that of sexual stimuli. Magazine pictures of women wearing low-cut blouses showing lots of cleavage drew an abnormal intensity of autonomic response from me. Because of that, I relished flipping through my sister's girlie magazines. Prior to the onset of the endocrinological malfunction, I was not so easily incited by sexually explicit material. Following the onset, even material that in normal circumstances would not be considered sexually explicit, elicited an autonomic response of abnormal intensity.

For a while, I tried to resist masturbating as I felt that it was morally wrong. After a few failed attempts I gave up as I was at the mercy of the invasive sexually explicit stimuli and together with the hypomanic state in which my sex drive had increased, the libido had to be satiated.

Anxiety

The endocrinological malfunction also had an adverse effect on anxiety. An analogy can be used to describe its effects. Anxiety when dormant is like a sleeping lion that has been chained up. The smell of fear (or metaphorically the smell of food) will agitate the anxiety (or the sleeping lion) and disturb its equilibrium (to awake the sleeping lion). In a panic attack situation, the lion has been disturbed sufficiently to prance around energetically. However, the lion is still being restrained by chains and can only prance about within its confined space.

With the endocrinological malfunction, there seemed to be less restraint on the anxiety (the lion had been freed from its chains). Although the cognitive reaction to the fearful situation was still equivalent to that of the normal person, the limited restraint on the anxiety made it difficult to control. I seemed to have lost my reins on the anxiety. Even though the anxiety did not elevate to the levels of a panic attack, the lack of control over it resulted in me succumbing to it. The anxiety controlled me more than I was able to control it. I was in a way a slave to anxiety. I did not have control over it and hence had to listen to it and follow it. In many circumstances, anxiety defined my actions.

One incident that happened early on in the onset of my newfound disabilities was during one of my oral examinations in primary school. I remember that I could hardly control the anxiety and that by the time the oral examination had started, I was disoriented and was relying more on my instinct and subconscious to deal with the situation. Likewise, in the years to come when faced with an anxious situation, for example giving presentations or even approaching to speak to my teacher or a member of the opposite sex, I was overcome by anxiety, could not think properly and had to rely on my subconscious to deal with the situation. I was never able to exert control on the anxious situation and the anxiety. This contrasted greatly to when I was younger. When I was younger, I remember that I relished telling stories in front of the class and I delighted in playacting in front of an audience. In the same way, I do not have any recollection of any fear of my teachers or members of the opposite sex. This anxiety or the lack of control over it seemed apparent only after the nightmare episode.

My inability to control my anxiety was one of the main reasons that subsequently resulted in my own self-reflection and realisation that I was dysfunctional. In so doing, it budded depression and related psychiatric illnesses. It was also the catalyst that spurred a steely determination to resolve my inefficacy.

Realisation

In my late teens and while in junior college, the realisation slowly struck me that I was dysfunctional. This transition period from adolescence to adulthood had brought about a new set of requirements for me to function adequately in society. No longer was I able to just engage in my pre-occupations and fritter away my time without any hopes and aspirations. My mentality was somehow still frozen in the period immediately following the onset of the increased serotonin and from thence had not matured much. I was consistently pre-occupied with a few stereotypical and restricted patterns of interest abnormal in intensity, meanwhile thriving in the false sense of happiness that included hyperactivity and elation. There was however little growth in my emotional maturity and little meaning to my life. Studying had become a routine without any purpose but only to fulfil an obligation. Life took on a dour facade without me being able to experience the whole range of sensibilities that defines a normal person.

It was at that time that the people around me started to mature and change. Their transformation was alien to me. Through my stunted sense and perception, I observed and envied the development of their emotional maturity and the hopes that came with their ambitions. Whilst my fellow schoolmates were planning for their future by applying for scholarships and entrance into prestigious universities, I could only clinically observe and understand their intentions but with an apathy not borne of choice but of disability. Because of this divergence of interests and maturities, I felt an inability to assimilate with my peers.

Prior to junior college, I was in an all-boys secondary school and had little interaction with the opposite sex. Junior college was where I had "closer" interaction with the opposite sex and where infatuations were not uncommon. However at that time I was not able to act on any of the infatuations because of a few reasons. The first of which was the inability to control anxiety and the second was my lack of sensibilities and shared interests. I displayed little commonality that could form the basis of a deeper relationship.

Depression

Gradually, as I came to realise my inadequacies and abnormalities, I grew depressed. Depression as generally understood results in the dysregulation of a number of neurotransmitter systems, including the serotonin, norepinephrine, dopamine, acetylcholine and gamma-aminobutyric acid systems. There is also evidence of alterations of several neuropeptides, including corticotropin-releasing hormone.

It was a compendium of sorts with an integrated and mixed set of symptoms pertaining to both depression and the endocrinological malfunction. It seemed as if the depression was now superimposed on the original endocrinological malfunction. Some effects were diminished while others magnified.

Hyperactivity and elation were now only apparent when there was a stimulus and even so were diminished and in a tainted form. Conversely, there was increased impairment in social and emotional empathy and reciprocity. Anxiety was still a considerable disability and in fact seemed to have magnified. Sense and awareness was subjected to greater impairment by the depersonalisation that was associated with anxiety and depression. Coupled with all these was that of the general dreary feeling characteristic of depression.

Life seemed even more meaningless now that the bouts of elation were less frequent and took on a lesser form. In short, my mood could be described as such: "A general gloom which was occasionally lifted by unnatural bouts of elation." I reckon that to a certain extent, the depression was offset partially by the increased serotonin from the endocrine system. However when stimulated by grandiose notions, mostly those of "victory", the serotonin (or opoid peptides) from the endocrine system, whose production had earlier been deregulated, would temporarily shoot up to offset and even surpass the effects of the depression. This led me to become quite convinced that I was suffering from manic depression. I subsequently recognised that I was mistaken, as my bouts of elation were milder and required some form of stimulus. This was quite different from the mania in manic depression, which is usually inexplicable, cyclical and needed no stimulus. Also because of the counteracting effects of the serotonin from the two different sources, the depression was not visibly apparent to most people. In fact, from my outward appearance and actions, most people did not notice that I was depressed.

Disturbances in the serotonin from two different sources complicated matters. If I were to depend on the current level of scientific knowledge within the medical fraternity, the increase in serotonin within the endocrine system would have to be considered as irreversible. With this initial complication, the subsequent reduction in serotonin resulting from the depression also became practically a lost cause. At some point in time, I realised that I could not be cured of the depression without first curing the fundamental problem of the increased serotonin within the endocrine system. This was because with the intensification of the serotonin within the endocrine system, the central nervous system failed to recognise the deficiency in its own production and was not able to modulate the serotonin that it produced to its natural levels.

The cure for general depression is to prod the patient into thinking positively and in so doing restore the serotonin in the central nervous system to its natural levels. In physiological terms, the pre-requisite for this is that the patient's central nervous system must first recognise that there is deficiency in the serotonin before stepping up production. Anti-depressants if applied correctly in quantity and regularity could be used as a catalyst to trigger this process. Conversely if applied wrongly, antidepressants may mislead the central nervous system into misjudging that there is no deficiency and this would prevent the serotonin levels from attaining its natural balance.

Sandwiched between the two physiological aberrations, I was in effect in a cul-de-sac. I knew that without first resolving the initial digression (endocrinological malfunction), I also could not resolve the subsequent deviation (depression).

Depersonalisation

My senses and awareness were already impaired by the initial onset of the increased serotonin. Depersonalisation that accompanied the depression led to me being further detached from my surroundings and the people around me. With depersonalisation, I had the sensation of being in a dream. I had become an outside observer of my mental processes, my physical body and the objects as well as the life forms around me. The world seemed mechanical and emotionless and I felt an even greater estrangement from people. I no longer knew how to relate to people and events. I felt uncomfortable and self-conscious in other people's presence, as I was no longer responsive to external stimuli including what people said, their actions, the happenings that occurred around me or even the specific events that I was a party to or was to be involved in. I had become an actor who did not comprehend the suitable response to the different situations of which I was both physically and emotionally estranged. As there was no commonality on which interactions could be based. I had to put on a false front and make up things to say to pretend that I was still in touch with reality. Usually what I said or did was contrived and sometimes untimely. This disability was apparent even when I was with my closest kin. I felt completely isolated.

Seeing the Specialists

As the realisation set in that I was dysfunctional and socially inept, it opened up a Pandora's box and I grew depressed. I was really stuck in a rut with the conflicting instinctive and cognitive needs and responses. Being depressed, I felt a numbness and lethargy that resulted in me not wanting to mix with people and taking part in social activities. Despite this, the hyperactivity and bouts of elation that still haunted me (albeit of a lesser form) continued to revel in purposeless activities that subjugated them. Moreover, because of the fear of being deemed socially inept in a world in which I felt isolated, I had the notion that I had to seem popular by continually being a party of the social activities that was typical of youth. In so doing, I could seem normal to my relatives and friends. This was an act because I was going for these social activities to upkeep and maintain an image and not because I really enjoyed them (especially now that the elation was tainted). There was little enjoyment because of both the physical and emotional detachment that accompanied the initial onset of the serotonin and the subsequent depression, and also because of the lethargy that came with the depression. I put on an act based on my limited scope of perception and understanding, the materials I collected from observing the actions of other people, and my understanding of life prior to the onset of the increased serotonin.

Festive seasons were the worst as my peers would have plans to go out to party with their friends. Conversely, I was stuck alone at home without anywhere to go. I did not want to appear to others that I had no "life". Yet, I was in a dilemma where in the depressed state I was not mentally up for any of these parties.

With the depression and the hopelessness there were suicidal tendencies but these were never strong urges as I was emotionally impassive and still "enjoyed" some of the vestiges of the hyperactivity and elation. It was within this hopelessness that I finally divulged to my family of my quandary. It was through my father that an appointment with a psychiatrist was made. I was so far detached and lacked motivation that if it depended on me I would not have the ability to make such an appointment. This action required a few steps. Firstly I had to know that there was such a thing as psychiatrists. Secondly it had to come to mind that there was a need for a psychiatrist. Thirdly I had to source for a psychiatrist. Lastly I had to endeavour to call the psychiatrist to make an appointment. I could not even get past the second step if I was to rely on myself. This was not a natural thought that could be borne of my narrow perception. The psychiatrist was the first of three psychiatrists and a neurologist that I was eventually introduced to. Although these practitioners did not assist much in my general medical condition and of which I felt an aversion towards because of their inadequacies, it was partially through my experience with them and the pickings of the crumbs of their knowledge that I eventually managed to unravel the puzzle.

The practitioners initially diagnosed my condition as general depression with a tinge of anxiety and social phobia. This conclusion was probably derived from my description of the depression and anxious episodes. One psychiatrist mentioned that this could be the result of me having to move from place to place when I was young. My father's work and overseas attachments required my family to be uprooted many times and I had to adapt to new schools and make new friends. With this frequent change of environment, I could have developed an "adjustment disorder". Others mentioned that my malady could be due to the stressful transition from adolescence to adulthood, during which I could not adapt to the changes in social requirements and it was the period of which for many, personality disorders surfaced. Their diagnosis was mostly about change and its effect on a person's social umbrella and his psyche.

The neurologist considered that I had a *schizoid personality disorder*. This conclusion was derived from my description of the pervasive pattern of detachment from social relationships and a restricted range of expression of emotions in interpersonal settings, beginning by early adulthood and present in a variety of contexts, including taking little pleasure in any activities, lacking close friends or confidants and emotional coldness, detachment and flattened affectivity. On hindsight, the neurologist may be correct if *schizoid personality disorder* is indeed an extension of the *autistic spectrum disorder*.

The psychiatrists prescribed me with antidepressants such as Zoloft and Prozac. Xanax was prescribed to me to reduce the anxiety. I took the medicine dutifully but they did not seem to have much effect on both depression and anxiety. After a considerable period of consultation with each psychiatrist, I realised that his/her applied treatment was ineffective and that he/she did not really understand my predicament. Each time, I decided to move on to seek a different opinion. All in all, I consulted three psychiatrists and a neurologist. The neurologist who diagnosed *schizoid personality disorder* told me that it was just my character and way of thinking, and that perhaps it was just my intelligence playing tricks on me. I was pretty sure he was wrong as I was certain that this was not my character and definitely not my real personality.

Research and Development

At about eighteen years of age, I started realising that I was different from others. I grew depressed at this knowledge that I was abnormal and knew that

I would never be able to assimilate into society, with this inability to manage both anxiety and hyperactivity. After visitations with various medical practitioners including psychiatrists and a neurologist, I was non-the-wiser as their diagnosis did not seem to pinpoint the actual problem. At that time, I also started to read up on related mental illnesses but none of those recorded seemed to fit my profile. The closest were attention deficit hyperactivity disorder (ADHD), anxiety disorders, manic-depression, *autism, asperger's syndrome* and personality disorders.

I knew that I had an anxiety disorder and depression, but I intuitively recognised that these were secondary effects of a more fundamental problem.

Initially I suspected that I was suffering from manic-depression. I subsequently recognised that I was mistaken, as my bouts of elation were milder and required some form of stimulus. This was quite different from the mania in manic depression, which is usually inexplicable, cyclical and needed no stimulus.

ADHD was discounted, as the symptoms of ADHD did not seem as disruptive to life as what I was suffering from. I also could not explain the difference between ADD and ADHD, with the former not showing the same hyperactivity symptoms as ADHD.

At that outset, *post traumatic stress disorder* (PTSD) did not seem likely as I did not at that time remember having recurrent flashbacks or dreams. Also there was no tangible event that happened that could have caused PTSD. For a moment, I pondered over whether the nightmare episode that I had encountered could have caused PTSD, but eventually PTSD was discounted as the direct associations of my symptoms with the nightmare episode were not obvious to me at that time because of the fragmentation of my memories.

As time passed I began to formulate the idea that my abnormality was not psychological, as the symptoms were not precipitated by my thoughts. Through this, I inferred that the cause was more likely physical. Personality disorders were discounted as I assumed such disorders are related to the person's psyche.

As I had the impression that my symptoms started only when I was around ten years of age, I inferred that this physical change had likely taken place during that period. That was also the period when the nightmare episode happened and strange physical symptoms appeared soon after.

At the outset, *autism* and *asperger's syndrome* did not seem likely as they were both associated with early stages of childhood development. As my affliction only started when I was about ten years old, I ruled them out as possible explanations.

Based on some knowledge I picked up on meditation and some information I obtained on the secondary "brain" known as the gut, I began to move my area of focus to the portion of the endocrine system along an imaginary path between the gut and the central nervous system. The method for the meditation which I was introduced to was to imagine an object moving along the path from the CNS to the gut. I surmised that this would aid to shift some of the chemicals from the CNS to the gut and vice versa, and reduce anxiety, one of which could be tryptophan. However, meditation can only work to reduce anxiety if the imbalance is temporary and not when it is permanent. It was along this path that I tried to design some physiotherapy that could permanently prevent the chemicals from moving between the gut to the CNS, but to no avail.

After a period of failure, I shifted my attention to the nether regions lying below the gut but that are extrapolations of the imaginary path. In effect, I was now focusing on the pelvic area. Eventually after a period of trial and error, I settled on the male genitalia as the likely suspect. It was when force was applied on specific areas of the male genitalia that some of the strange physical symptoms that I had encountered when I was ten years old resurfaced. At that time however the physiotherapy was still primitive and ineffective.

It was through God's grace that I eventually identified the exact location that was the culprit to my anomaly. It is this area where I guess the inflammation of the serotogenic neurons had taken place and had become an unwanted source of serotonin. It was also through God's grace that I identified the methodology that was highly effective to overcome this affliction. The location had to be precise and the methodology exact. Any small deviations would render the physiotherapy ineffective. It is expected though that the medical fraternity will in future devise a more progressive and effective method of physiotherapy.

At this point I still had no clue as to the terminology of my illness. It was God's direction that brought me upon the knowledge of the physical effects of excess serotonin. Subsequently it was also brought to my attention that some studies had shown that *autism* had connections with serotogenic dysfunction. Further information on the physical side effects of *autism* confirmed my suspicions. These physical side effects of *autism* were similar to those that I experienced. With this confirmation, I became certain that I was suffering from a disorder that was on the same spectrum as *autism* and *asperger's syndrome*.

Through the plotting of my condition along a time scale reflecting the onset of the disorder, it dawned on me that *autism* and *asperger's syndrome* did not necessarily originate from birth or even during the early stages of a child's development.

If *autism* and *asperger's syndrome* did not necessarily originate from birth, there must be a continuous spectrum on which both these disorders lie. I began to wonder which disorder constituted the other end of the spectrum. I recalled reading some material on the chronic effects of PTSD. Coupled with this was the nightmare episode that seemed to have triggered my condition. Putting the two together, I realised that the chronic physiological effects of PTSD may lie on the other end of the spectrum.

If *autism, asperger's syndrome* and the chronic physiological effects of PTSD are on the same spectrum of disorders, there has to be an explanation for the differences in symptoms. I hypothesised that the differences were due to the age of onset of the endocrinological malfunction. The age of onset decided the extent of impairment on the victim's developmental skills and the probability of mental retardation.

The difficulty now is to convince the medical fraternity of my findings. I hope that those who read this material will be open-minded because this is indeed a big discovery.

The After Effect

Every time I carry out the physiotherapy, there is a sustained period of abnormal moods and physical symptoms. The degree of the abnormal moods and physical symptoms depends on the effectiveness of the physiotherapy. The more effective the physiotherapy, the greater the altercations in mood. The after-effect of the physiotherapy usually lasts for a period of about a year, gradually lessening in intensity. This period is torturous as it is a period of uncertainty, ever-changing moods and wracking migraine headaches. The dissipation of the after-effect takes place gradually and is not abrupt.

After carrying out the physiotherapy, hypomania sets in almost immediately. Sometimes this hypomania can reach the heights of mania, during which cognition may be impaired.

In my final few therapy sessions, by which time I had already discovered the key to its effectiveness, I applied the methods with efficacy and this led to intensification of the symptoms of the after-effect. It is construed that the physiotherapy if carried out effectively, results in a sharp decline of the serotonin production from the endocrine system. Consequently, the CNS reacts to the sharp decline by rapidly increasing its own serotonin production. However, the CNS, working like a rusty machinery suddenly being put into action, is not able to regulate the serotonin output properly and unable to immediately find a suitable equilibrium. This inability to find the natural equilibrium results in fluctuations in the levels of serotonin in different parts of the brain, which can lead to interchanging bouts of mania and depression. The extent of this mania can be illustrated by some happenings that occurred during my bouts of after-effect.

In some cases of extreme mania, cognition has been impaired to such an extent that reality is significantly altered. In the throes of mania, some people have developed grandiose notions that are very far from reality. For example, there are manic people who think that they are the incumbent president or even God. These people start to act out the role that they have assumed in their altered reality. Some people even experience hallucinations.

Even though my mania was pretty severe, it was not severe enough to impair my cognition to the point where it was obvious that I was irrational. No matter what are the heights of my mania, I am sure I would not think of myself as God as I do not have supernatural powers and in my own self-rationalisation of my sinful nature, I do not have the nobility borne of God.

Despite my intelligence and usually rational behaviour, the mania did alter my sense of reality. I had grandiose notions of being a successful entrepreneur and a stock market guru. In my mind, I started formulating countless business ideas. There were those related to the food industry, finance industry and even those related to religiosity. Most of these business ideas were unrealistic. However I must say that some of the ideas were highly creative and the few practical ones could perhaps bear some fruits if efforts are put in.

Thinking that I was a stock market guru, I started to actively research into equities and their fundamentals. The mania induced me to have unrealistic expectations of the future performance of the equities. When I studied the financial reports of some of the firms I was keen in investing in, I had over-optimistic projections of their future performance. At one point, I was so certain of my forecast of their future performance that I started pumping loads of funds into the equities I had selected for my portfolio. Reality hit me hard as the performances of the equities were way off my expectations. For example there was one stock where I had projected a 50 percent increase in their earnings. The actual result was close to a 30 percent reduction in their earnings. This was indeed a significant margin of error.

The mania almost led me into an affair that could have had severe repercussions and ruin many peoples' lives. In the manic state, I had exorbitant ideas that I was particularly attractive to women and that they could not possibly resist me.

I had a female colleague who is five years my senior. When I first started work at the government transportation agency, she was already with one child. During that time, I never did fathom having a romantic interest in her or even thought about her sexually. I could not imagine being interested in a woman who is so much older than me. Moreover as she is married and with one child, it is definitely not righteous to indulge in any thoughts of a covetous or sexual nature. If someone were to tell me then that I would fall in love with her or even possibly have an affair with her, I would deem it as absolutely absurd and ridiculous.

This colleague of mine has a pleasant and bubbly personality. She is also very helpful and compassionate. If she knows a person well, she is very frank with what she says and sometimes divulges very personal and intimate details that are more appropriate for a close confidante. She is also very helpful and would go all out of her way to help others.

There was a period when she started to dress better, with a significant change in her outlook and appearance. This was a period when we started to work closely together. Being a sufferer of hyperthyroidism, perhaps it was her elevated moods that induced her to pay more attention to her outward appearance.

Under mania's deception, I misinterpreted her sharing of intimate information and changes in her appearance to be signals that she had developed a liking for me. This thought persisted for some time and it gradually ignited my curiosity. Adding fuel to the fire was problems in my own relationship. There was also considerable respect and admiration for her helpful and compassionate character. Overtime, I developed affection for her.

During her pregnancy with her second child and in the midst of the aftereffect of my physiotherapy, I could not leash my curiosity and mania anymore and asked her whether she had developed feelings for me. I told her that because I had the perception that she had feelings for me, I couldn't help but reciprocate and the affection was growing. That was when things started to get out of hand......

I have now come to regret some of the things I have done while I was in my manic state. Even though I have made significant losses on the stock market, fortunately for me the losses were still bearable. In fact as of this date, I have more than recovered on my losses. Although I almost got myself into a tumultuous relationship, I did not go beyond the boundaries that would have had severe repercussions. I am thankful that even in times of mania, God has kept me in check and continued to protect me. He has in His own way lessened the impact and consequences of my altered perceptions.

Taking this step to write this book is a step of faith. I sometimes wonder whether I have made the right decision as my thoughts could have been influenced by mania and writing this book could just be one of the grandiose themes typical of mania. However, God has shown me many signs that it is in His will that I write this book. I hope that I have not in my manic state misinterpreted these signs. I am sure however that this book will help many who have suffered and despaired in the same way that I have over the years.

As the mania gradually diminishes, depression starts to set in. At some stage both mania and depression would co-exist concurrently and they would surface one after another in an alternating fashion. While the depression is more prominent during the daytime, the hypomania usually takes charge at night. This fluctuation generally followed the pattern of a circadian cycle but was not necessarily so as there could be days when I felt depressed the whole day while other days I could be entirely hypomanic.

Both the depression and mania would lessen until the neuro-endocrinological condition reaches its semi-permanent equilibrium. The CNS will eventually find its natural equilibrium. However along the way, because of the fluctuation of serotonin from the CNS, mania and depression will alternate.

Many of the symptoms of the after-effect appeared to correlate with the fluctuation of serotonin levels. The steep transition from mania to hypomania and from hypomania to normalcy was accompanied by memory loss. From the peaks of the mania to the lesser highs of hypomania, there was significant memory loss of prior events that occurred during the manic state. The manic state was like a dream and in the same way as dreams are easily forgotten, things that happened in the preceding days did not leave much of an impression on my mind. Perhaps the increase in serotonin from the endocrine system also plays an important part in the dissociative amnesia commonly found in trauma victims. Dissociative amnesia is significant memory loss of the traumatic event or things that happened shortly after the event. During the traumatic event, the acute stress could have triggered an increased production of serotonin and its sudden surge and subsequent reduction could have temporarily impaired the retention of memory in the temporal lobe. This would cause trauma victims to forget the details of the traumatic experience.

This roller-coaster effect of serotonin also led to other physical symptoms. These physical symptoms include migraine headaches, gastrointestinal disturbances, increased flatulence, eczema and muscle twitching. The migraine headaches were similar to the hangover experienced after a period of being high on drugs or alcohol. During this period, the immune system was sometimes also suppressed and there was an increased tendency to catch influenza or fever. Other symptoms include an ache on the forehead (this ache felt more like a muscle ache then a headache). Sometimes after waking up from deep sleep, there were wrinkles on my body and numbness, especially of my limbs.

I also encountered a few bouts of aggression during the manic-depressive period. The depressive state was sometimes associated with aggression. On one recent occasion, because of a small misunderstanding with my mother, we got into an argument. I cannot remember any other occasions when I have felt so angry. In fact, most of my life I have never felt truly angry. Even if I did feel irritated or frustrated, my anger was always mild. The argument grew heated and when my mother in her fury told me that my book would never be a success, I was totally incensed and demanded that she stop the car in the middle of nowhere so that I could get off the car. I was actually surprised at my own demands; it did not seem typical of my usually meek disposition.

Flashbacks

I remember that shortly after the initial nightmare episode, I had a few recurrent nightmares of the same nature. However, for a long time since then, I have not had similar nightmares. Even dreams are infrequently recalled.

Midway through the physiotherapy, there was once again a period of recurrence of nightmares that were similar to the nightmare episode that I had encountered when I was ten years old. These nightmares were of a similar nature but could take on different forms. While the original nightmare was one where my family had changed into malevolent apparitions, one recent nightmare was about my family undergoing altercations into aliens. Some others were about me being trapped or pursued by malevolent beings.

The sudden emergence of these nightmares seems to indicate that the removal of the effects of the endocrinological malfunction has uncovered the consolidated memory of the trauma. This seems to point towards the endocrinological malfunction serving its function as a "protective mechanism" that keeps these intrusive memories under wraps. After a few episodes of these nightmares, my dream world has returned to normal and once again obscure. I hardly remember any of my dreams nowadays.

5

My Personal Testimony

The period of my life during which I had to contend with the ravages of my malady can be divided into three distinct periods. The first period was since the onset of the illness from when I was about ten years old to about eighteen years old. The subsequent period was from eighteen years old, the period when the realisation struck me that I was dysfunctional, to about twenty-four years old. This was a period of uncertainty, hopelessness and depression. My attempts to isolate the problem and treat myself then were futile, wayward and ineffective.

I was twenty-four years old when I came to know God and was baptised in the same year. For me, it was a new life and a new beginning. Even though there was no change in my physical limitations, knowing and accepting God as my personal saviour brought fresh hope to my battered and bruised psyche. As I placed every facet of my limitations into God's hands faithfully, God opened up a path for me. With the guidance of the Holy Spirit in my endeavours, in due course, I isolated the source of my troubles and even learnt how to cure it. This was not something that I could have done if based on my own abilities. It was during this period, that I was frequently fluctuating in and out of the after-effects of the physiotherapy I had devised. However each time the after-effects dissipated, I was a step closer to normalcy.

This period lasted for quite a while. The physiotherapy helped but unfortunately the process was slow. There was still a missing element. It was not until later that I realised the importance of masturbation as part of the physiother-

60

apy that it became more effective. I am now twenty-eight years old and am almost fully recovered.

During the first period of my autistic experience, I was oblivious to my disability. I revelled in the hyperactivity and the elation that was derived from the few interests that I had. I still managed to assimilate with my peers as some of these interests were shared and I had at least ten years of prior normality that contributed to some commonality.

The turning point occurred when I was about eighteen years old. This was the period when my peers matured and set their sights on higher aspirations. I was still trapped within my restricted patterns of interest that were immature and less appropriate for my age. It was then that I realised that I was different and as a result I grew depressed.

At that point, I had lost all hope and knew that if nothing was done, I was faced with no meaning in my life. Despite all this, I still managed to do well for my GCE "A" levels, the entry examinations for university. I scored 4As in my core subjects and distinctions in both my "special" papers (papers that are considered much more difficult than the normal papers). This was quite a feat considering the difficulties that I was facing. These results were good enough to apply for any scholarships that were available. However with my mental imbalance and immaturity, I flunked the solitary scholarship interview that I went for. I remember spouting some nonsense at the interview when the interviewers queried why I had not applied for entry into any of the prestigious universities. In response to their query, I replied that I had some personal problems but was unable to explain what it was all about because of its confidentiality. In effect, I was setting my own death sentence by making such a statement. It was also partially because of my excellent results that medical practitioners refused to believe that I had any major psychiatric illness.

The next phase of my life was to enter two and a half years of compulsory military service. I was downgraded to "unfit for combat" based on the doctors' diagnosis of generalised anxiety disorder and was assigned a role as a clerk in the army. The doctors had underestimated the severity of my condition. This was equivalent to diagnosing pneumonia as a common cold.

I was to go for regular consultations at the psychiatric ward at the Old Changi Hospital. The ward was a depressing site with doors looking like that of a prison cell. Once I entered the ward, the iron grilled doors were locked after me and I was left waiting in the ward with the other patients, some of whom were only there for consultation, while others were there to stay. After my first consultation, I ceased to go there any longer as I felt that I was very much treated like a prisoner.

Unless you entered the officer cadet school and became an army officer, the army was a place where the "regular" servicemen reigned supreme. Those national servicemen who were completing their obligation (of two to two and the half years of national service) in fulfilling their national duty had to be subject to the "regular" servicemen's whims and fancy. This was more a result of the system where you had little choice of an alternate employer. Of course, in the army, you had to be disciplined and follow the line of command. After completing my basic military training, I was posted to an artillery unit as a clerk. The chief clerk was an Indian female "regular" who frequently had mood swings and blew her top at the slightest of errors made by her subordinates. Being unmarried, it was a mixture of her loneliness (hormonal imbalances), perception that national servicemen were a lazy, obnoxious lot and her excessive power over us that made her out to be what she was to be.

During that time, many of us lived in torrid fear. In the prisons of my *autism*, I was not able to exhibit any defiance and could only dutifully obey and abide. Yet, no one medical practitioner was able to verify the extent of my condition and relieve me of some of the ardour of army life. Fortunately for me, perhaps because of my intelligence, I could easily complete the systematic duties without much error and was usually spared from brushes with her temperament. Additionally, my job scope required careful detail and accuracies in conforming to fixed processes. This fitted in nicely with my pedantic nature and my inclination towards routines. When I completed my stint in the army, my Certificate of Service recorded me as having both an outstanding conduct and performance.

In the army, I found it even more difficult to adapt to the people as they were from all walks of life. The divide was exacerbated with these background differences adding to my social impairment. My unit required us to stay in, meaning that we were allowed to go out at night but had to return by 11 p.m.

It was during these moments that I was at my greatest disarray and misery. Whereas clerical work was continuous during the day and became an easily followed routine, the nights were a break in routine that I was not able to manage. With the potent mix of *autism* and depression, I did not know what to do during these breaks. With the social impairment and depression, I was not able to assimilate with my fellow colleagues and did not regularly hang out with them. Even if I attempted to do sometimes, I was very uncomfortable and had to put up a false front. With no meaning and aim in life, I did not make use of the time to do anything constructive such as taking night lessons or driving lessons. I also did not stay in the camp because of my hyperactivity and the prideful side of me not wanting people to make me out to be a desolate loner. My nights were hence divided between sometimes going home and sometimes wandering around aimlessly without any purpose.

Home was a distance away and the travelling time to-and-fro took about two and half-hours. The remaining time I had to rest at home and eat dinner was less than two hours. Despite the inconvenience of going home, I still did so on most days. It was the place where I was most comfortable, where there were no anxieties and where I could follow my usual restricted routine without the fear of being judged by people.

Sometimes my fears gave in to reason and I berated myself for being weak and irrational by succumbing to the comfort zone of my home. It was times like this that I attempted to go around on my own. I would look for a place near my camp to have dinner but yet frequently when about to enter the eatery, I would take a step back in fear that someone from my unit would recognise me and notice me eating alone. There was this fear that I would be judged to be abnormal and a recluse. So often it was that I wandered from eatery to eatery in search of the most esoteric location where I could have my dinner in peace and without the anxieties. After dinner and without any purpose, I continued to wander around aimlessly. I did not want to return to my camp too early and let people realise that I had no plans, which would showcase my peculiarities and my emptiness.

Two years in the artillery unit passed without much progress in my condition. Despite that, I did my best to remain positive. Even though I was well wedged in the state of oblivion, I still had to get on with life. The obvious next step was to go to university. In July 1997, I started my course of study in Engineering in the National University of Singapore. The same issues of difficulty assimilating with my course mates surfaced. Now that I was deeper into the depression, the hyperactivity and bouts of elation were of a lesser form and more tainted. Some of my course mates were friends that I had known a few years back in Raffles Junior College. Despite my familiarity with them, the autistic tendencies and depression made me feel out of place even with them and I had to constantly put on a false front to appear normal. I told some closer friends about my problem but it was difficult for me to explain, as there were no references to be drawn from. As of that time, I did not yet know its relation with *autism*. Even if I did, it was a hopeless cause, as there was no cure for *autism*.

Midway through my studies, my devout Buddhist mom was introduced to a supposed venerable monk that could cure me of my affliction. I was resistant to taking part in the rites but as my mom insisted, I was powerless to do anything to dissuade her in my oblivious state. The monk explained that the metaphysical world followed the principles of "cause" and "effect". What is happening in the present is the consequence of what has happened in the past or during your past life. It was hence necessary to chant sutras to please the "gods" and submit offerings to the "spirits", to appease them. This would change the course of fate I was told. I had to go through three days of intensive chanting and kow-towing. Each day, I had to kow-tow hundreds of times.

In this way, we parted with an equivalent of sixty thousand U.S. dollars. This was given to the dodgy monk for his preparations and personal remuneration.

As I expected, despite having gone through all the rituals, I did not feel any different. It was not effective as the monk claimed. The sixty thousand U.S. dollars had gone down the drain. Seeing that the rituals did not help me, my mom had no choice but to explore other avenues. On one night, she prayed to Jesus and told Him that although she did not know Him and found it hard to imagine and follow Him, she hoped that He would help me. Immediately following this claim of His might and glory, different groups of my mother's friends started to approach her to attend their church services. It was when I accompanied her for one of these church services that I got to know a pastor who followed up with me on weekly biblical lessons that I eventually came to accept Jesus as my personal saviour.

One of the verses that struck me then was Psalm 23:4, as follows:

"Even though I walk through the valley of the shadow of death, I will fear no evil, for you are with me; your rod and your staff, they comfort me."

This was the promise that God had made to us through His Word. I was certainly walking through the valley of the shadow of death and God had promised to take care of my needs while I was still lingering in the throes of despair. I took faith at God's promise and was certain that God would lead me out of my misery. With renewed hope, I continued exploring the physiotherapy that I had devised, certain that it was God's promise to me of my recovery.

Initially, the physiotherapy helped but the process was slow. Improvement was apparent but gradual. Somehow every time I thought I had effectively completed the whole process, once the after-effects of the physiotherapy subsided, the effects of the autistic disorder and depression still lingered, despite being somewhat diminished. It was really frustrating, as I had put in substantial efforts in the physiotherapy and was subject to the barrages of the torturous after-effect, but yet, I was not completely healed.

It was only recently that I realised that the key to unlocking the effectiveness of the physiotherapy is masturbation. It is necessary that masturbation is carried out together with the physiotherapy and in an orderly fashion. Putting my new discovery into action, I am glad to say that I am now almost fully recovered.

During my stint in university, I did not do well in my studies by my own standards. I managed a second class (lower) honours degree in Mechanical Engineering. I did well for the first year, but in the subsequent years my studies deteriorated for a few reasons. Firstly, I was disillusioned with life and felt that there was no purpose in getting good grades. Secondly, the barrages of the after-effects of the physiotherapy wore me down both mentally and physically. Added to that was the time-consuming needs of the difficult relationship I got myself into. Last but not least was a poor grade in my Final Year Project that made the difference between second class (upper) and second class (lower) honours degree.

My Final Year Project was titled "Design and Development of Composite Orthodontic Brackets". Orthodontic brackets are the part of the braces that are attached to the teeth. After doing substantial research, I found that with my resources back then, limited scope of knowledge and time span of less than a year, it was not feasible for me to design and develop any useful composite orthodontic bracket that was unique and different from those on the market. Those composite brackets on the market were not really effective and compared poorly in performance with metallic and ceramic brackets. It was highly possible that the project was a wild goose chase with unrealistic goals and assumptions. I tried to seek guidance from my supervisor who was then the vice-dean of Engineering. He was ever so busy with his climb up the corporate ladder and was supervising so many projects that he had little time left for me. I felt that in his pursuit of his own selfish desires and ambitions, he was not fulfilling his duties as a mentor and a teacher. That was how he subsequently became dean of Engineering. These are the cruel realities of life.

It is noted that great discoveries are not unravelled in short periods of time of less than a year. I was also a victim of the educational system that did not encourage inventiveness and only rewarded those who conformed to the Norm. It was only by conforming to the Norm that one could produce results in the Final Year Project that can substantiate a better grade. By attempting new things, it was not likely that results can be produced within one year and that would also be reflected as a poor grade.

My own discoveries in *autism* had taught me not to conform to the Norm. It was with this attitude that I took on the Final Year Project. As a result, I fared poorly.

In the movie "Beautiful Mind", John Nash was portrayed as someone who wanted to do something distinct and unique. Initially in Princeton, he could not produce results that would ensure his professorship in a prestigious college because he did not want to conform to the Norm. Fortunately for him, he eventually managed to do so and in his autumn years was even awarded with the Nobel Prize.

Even as I was in my oblivious state in university, girls still found me attractive. Perhaps it was my boyish good looks or the mysterious aura that surrounded me that was accentuated by me often looking apprehensive and deep in thought. Initially, I had little interaction with girls, as I did not take part in any social activities. It was only during my second year in the university that I took part in a freshman orientation camp as a senior. It was during this camp that I was acquainted with some girls. There were the more brash ones who made it obvious to you of their interest, while there were the shy ones who were subtle in their display of their fondness.

My preference was for the more docile girls. However, at that point I was very firm that I would not enter into a relationship because of my own uncertainties. There seemed little hope for me to be able to lead a normal life. I also felt that it would be near impossible to establish any meaningful relationship with my disabilities.

Time passed and I learnt of the might and the glory of God. As I learnt more about Jesus and His sacrifices, I accepted Him as my personal saviour. I learnt to depend on the Holy Spirit to guide me in every aspect of my life. The Holy Spirit is a miraculous entity and if we are willing and submissive, the Holy Spirit frequently intervenes in our life for our best interests. It was the works of the Holy Spirit that gave me an insight into my affliction.

As *autism* is an affliction where there is impairment in communication skills, I hardly talked to the girls face-to-face. It was only through the ICQ (I seek you) that I got to know the girls better. The ICQ was a faceless internet communication channel through which I could convey my deepest thoughts. It allowed communication in a relaxed environment without me having to feel uncomfortable in the presence of another person. It also allowed me to take my time to respond and to craft my replies to be politically correct. This limited any first-time awkward responses that are symptomatic of *autism*.

Two girls from my orientation camp stood out from the rest. They were both good friends of one another. Somehow both of them fell deeply in love with me. One of them folded a thousand paper cranes for me without my knowledge. The other folded a hundred paper cranes for me and gave them to me. I do not know what the thing with paper cranes is, but to them it was an expression of love. Initially, I was resistant to their affection. I knew that I was not in the correct frame of mind to be in a relationship. I also knew that what I knew of "love" now would be different from what I would know of "love" if I was to be healed eventually. There is a difference in the feelings of "love" when one is in the throes of the emotional apathy of autism. I also felt that if I were to make a choice then, it would not be my best choice, as it would be a choice restricted by my inadequacies and passiveness.

The girl who folded the hundred paper cranes turned up at the baptism ceremony on the day I was to be baptised. On that day, the Holy Spirit softened my heart and conditioned it to be more accepting of a relationship. I felt that it was God's will that I enter into this relationship. I decided to focus on the present rather than the uncertain future. One month later, I got attached to this same girl.

The relationship was not without difficulties. Being autistic, I was hardly mindful of romance and showed little care and concern. On the other hand, my girlfriend had struggles with low self-esteem and social phobia and anxieties. Because of her low self-esteem, she had the need to feel loved, treasured and vindicated. This was not something I could provide as I was in an emotionally apathetic state with an imaginary wall separating me from my close ones. Moreover I was too preoccupied with my own struggles that I did not pay heed to her needs. With these differences, there were many quarrels and unhappiness. There were many times when quarrels ended with no clear consensus and conclusive agreement. I felt really stifled particularly by her possessiveness and unreasonable behaviour. Many times when I was on my way to taking part in activities that excluded her, she felt neglected and kicked up a big ruckus. This was especially so when there were acquaintances of the opposite sex jointly taking part in these activities. It was worse when she perceived them as having a liking for me. This really affected my mood and dampened my spirits for the otherwise enjoyable activities.

I admit though that I had some part to play in her insecurities. Because of my emotional estrangement, I failed to do my part as a boyfriend and did not even accompany her to the clinic to give her emotional support even as she had her lasik eye surgery. I frequently played down the necessity of having to be romantic. I often complained about the need to buy presents for special occasions and grumbled over the price of roses during Valentine's Day. This is something I regret, but I felt it was no excuse for her unreasonable behaviour. It was a behaviour that bespoke of psychological instability and to me it was a pre-cursor of an unhappy marriage if I was to eventually wed her.

Other than not showing care and concern, another of my girlfriend's major complaint was that I hardly showed any affection. During the initial periods of courtship, I did show some affection and there was some physical intimacy. After the initial "euphoria" of romantic love, I resumed my staid nature and was lacklustre when it came to showing any affection and physical intimacy. It has been a long time since I initiated any hugging or kissing. I also have a dislike for holding hands as I find it uncomfortable and argue that it restricts my freedom. This aversion towards touch is symptomatic of *autism*.

Despite all these difficulties, we are still together. God is changing her gradually. Even though there has been many quarrels and unhappiness, I thank God that He had provided her to me to support me throughout my struggles with the debilitating after-effects of the physiotherapy. Despite her shortcomings, she did provide me with much needed company and a listening ear that is much appreciated. At this point, our future together is however uncertain as I am not sure what "love" is anymore. Her unreasonable behaviour has eroded most of my original love and respect for her. I hope that as God changes her, I will rediscover my love and respect for her and that this love will evolve from the original romantic love "Eros" that is frequently transient to the long-lasting love of "Agape". Furthermore, I also have some reservations as to whether I could have made a better choice if I was not abnormal back then. Nevertheless, if it is in God's purpose for us to be together, I hope that God will teach me to love her. I will henceforth surrender my relationship to God and place everything into His hands as He can do no wrong.

A point to note is that love is defined by a person's sense and awareness of another person. If there is a change to the person's sense and awareness as the person recovers from *autism*, the basis of the original love has changed and there is a corresponding change in the love that the person feels for the other person. I notice that prior to the onset of *autism*, I was particularly attracted to girls that are slightly plump. During the autistic state, I preferred slimmer girls. My girlfriend is also of the "slim" category. As I am coming out of the *autism* now, my preference for plumper girls seems to have temporarily revived. It is however too early to conclude whether that is of any long-term significance to my future choices.

Recently I almost had an affair with a colleague. It was a ludicrous state of affairs that if it had not happened, I would not have possibly imagined it. As I already have a girlfriend, I am usually guarded when conversing with other female acquaintances so as not to create any fatal attractions. However this colleague was different as she was married with one kid and she is five years older than me. It was when I was with her that I let my guard down as I felt that it was not possible between us. Initially I had some suspicions that she liked me as there were a few occasions when she stayed back late coincidentally when I had to do overtime. She also started to dress up and changed her hairstyle to look prettier and younger. Because I felt that she liked me and because she is a really jovial and very helpful character, I gradually started to fall for her. My perception that she liked me was like a seed that started to take root in my mind and that was to be watered by other events that were taking place. Being a Christian and one who abhorred immorality, I began to take a defensive stance and frequently spoke harshly to her. Because of my harshness, she started to eat-in during lunch hours in a bid to avoid me.

When my liking for her was still a seedling, God had already warned me through prophetic means that I was treating things too trivially and in doing so I was being irresponsible. In the same prophetic message, God warned me that I was to follow the decrees He had set in the bible. I knew that God was referring to this matter. Tears welled up in my eyes as I understood God's message. At that time, I treated this matter trivially as I did not feel that it would get out of hand. As it later seemed to be going a little out of control, I tried to do the responsible thing and decided to clear things up with her. At first, I messaged her using my hand phone to ask her whether she liked me. As she denied it fervently, I told her that I felt that she had feelings for me and coupled with her being a really nice person, there was a tendency for me to reciprocate. I continued that even though this was not really the case as she had stated, we should try to avoid each other to prevent any repercussions.

Immediately following my disclosures, her lunching pattern changed. The past few weeks had seen her eating-in. Now, she suddenly reverted back to lunching with me and my other colleagues. This reinforced my suspicions that her eating-in had something to do with me. There was one fine day when I had to walk to the local post office quite some distance away from my work office to make my new driving license after lunch. I was pleasantly surprised when she offered to accompany me to the post office as she was already in the final stage of pregnancy with her second child. Even though I myself did not ever experience pregnancy, I knew that the impetus had to be quite substantial for her to walk such a lengthy distance with considerable weight in her womb. The only reason that I could conceive was "love".

As I became more and more convinced that she loved me, the thought of her being in love with me continued to gnaw on my mind daily. It came to a point when I had to confirm my suspicions. One day when she was on her maternity leave after bearing her second child, I let loose through electronic messaging that I had developed some feelings for her. It was part of my strategy to gauge her response and confirm my suspicions. I told her that even though it was not possible between us, we could at least be truthful to one another. Once again, she vehemently denied her liking for me. Thinking that what she was telling me was to be the truth and that I had to have some way to channel my feelings, I asked her whether I could take her as a sister, which she agreed. At that point, I thought that I could finally lay the matter to rest. As long as I knew that she had no romantic interest in me, I did not feel the need to reciprocate and my romantic feelings would die down naturally.

When she came back from her maternity leave, I felt a little awkward, but thought that the situation would revert back to normal and that we could still be good friends and as close as siblings. It came as a little surprise when she told me that she was losing control over herself and her feelings for me. That also re-ignited my romantic feelings for her. There was no turning back......

We were almost out of control as the passion filled and incensed us. God's prophetic message to me was to follow the decrees He had set in the bible. In the bible, God's stand against adultery was obvious. Passion had already consumed my personal stand on morality. Passion had also made me blind to the dire consequences on the many people around us if we were to establish a romantic relationship. There would not only be psychological repercussions on her husband, her children and my girlfriend, our family and friends would also look down on us. It was also a really bad testimony of God's name to my family and associates. The only thing that had some effect in holding me back from adultery was God's word. Even then the passion had almost consumed me. It was difficult for me to reconcile such pure love with God's rules and regulations. "Love" was supposed to be good and yet in this instance, it was regarded as a sinful act. At one point I was really dissatisfied with God for allowing such a conflict.

Fortunately for me, I had a God fearing pastor who really loved God and abided by His words. At my wits ends, I divulged my unfaithfulness to my girlfriend and together with her we sought my pastor's help and counselling. My girlfriend was aggrieved by my confessions and yet I could not reassure her that I still loved her. My pastor prayed for us and counselled us. Overtime and with lots of efforts, I eventually overcame the temptations.

I felt that I had little control over the situation and somewhat blamed God for putting me in a situation where I could not fend for myself. I reasoned that I had fallen into this temptation because of a few factors. Firstly, I was under the after-effects of the excess serotonin during the period following the physiotherapy. The excess serotonin made me unclear and hyperactive to the point of being manic. Parallels can be drawn to being "high" on drugs or alcohol. It was during the periods of "high" that I had little restraint on my own thoughts and actions. The second reason was because of the unhappiness in my own relationship. I was really put off by my girlfriend's unreasonable behaviour and its repetition had conceived a resistance and distaste that I felt towards her. The third reason was because I had always thought that my colleague had feelings for me and because she is of really good character despite her moral failings, I felt the tendency to reciprocate. She also provided a stark contrast to my girlfriend and I could see in her the many virtues that were absent in my girlfriend.

The fourth reason is a little more abstract. I felt that there was also a relation to Oedipus complex. I was around ten years old when I experienced the nightmare episode that resulted in imagined separation from my mother. Despite the reality being different, the physiological effects had set in. The physiological effects played a part in masking the psychological effects of the separation and hence it was never quite removed. It was possible that as I was being cured from *autism*, the vacuum became more apparent and it resulted in an attraction towards the expectant mother, which was sought to fill up the vacuum.

During my initial struggles with *autism*, I had always been pessimistic about my ability to find and hold down meaningful employment. Even if I managed to secure meaningful employment, I was pretty sure I would not be able to perform well at work. Being effective at your workplace required the ability to conceptualise things well, emotional intelligence a.k.a. social empathy, as well as communication and presentation skills.

It was with some apprehension that I sent out my resumes. I was not selective, as my confidence levels were low in being able to secure a job. I would have been happy as long as I was able to get past the interviews and start work as soon as possible. Interviews were a problem, as I could not control my anxiety well. Frequently at interviews my inability to leash the anxiety created in me a state of oblivion, and I had to rely on my subconscious and pre-prepared answers to gloss over the disability. I also had no good answers to various questions on why I did not apply for scholarship and why I was downgraded to medically unfit in the army.

After being called up for seven interviews, it was with God's grace that I managed to secure two job offers. One of them was for an R&D position in electronics giant Philips and the other was a position as a transportation safety engineer in the civil service. I chose the latter because of its proximity to my home and it seemed more interesting.

Fortunately for me, my initial work involved mostly the writing of reports and papers, with little need for verbal communication and presentations. I managed to impress my superiors as the nature of my work played on my strong points and did not highlight my social and verbal impairment and weaknesses.

The first year also saw me start a seven-month stint as the secretary of a management meeting that was held weekly and chaired by the deputy chief executive. The meeting was held to discuss project implementation issues and approve various project expenditures. The issues discussed at the meeting were wide-ranging and involved aspects that included regulatory, contractual, financial, insurance, architecture, safety, programme planning and civil/electrical/mechanical engineering. This was one of the most difficult periods of my life, as I was still new to the organisation and did not have an inkling of most of these issues. Other than carrying out my own work, I had to read all the pre-meeting papers, make all the administrative/logistical meeting arrangements and prepare the meeting minutes.

Preparation of the minutes was most difficult. With my lack of sensory integration, it was difficult for me to listen to the discussion at the meeting and understand its content at the same time. It was as if my thoughts were one step slower than what was being said. Moreover, I had little knowledge of the background of what was being discussed. My adaptive ability had to once again be put to good use as I would jot down every single word that I could hear, often without understanding, and piece them together after the meeting.

When more than one person spoke at any one time, I also found it difficult to focus on the pertinent conversation. Frequently, I would miss out something that was said during the meeting, I would call up other people who attended the meeting to check with them their version of what was being said.

Most of the time it was a guessing game as I tried to piece together all the bits of information that I had heard to form a logical story. My inability to control anxiety was also a liability as I was frequently close to the state of oblivion when I was taking down the minutes during the meeting. Because of the intense and uncontrolled anxiety, I was usually exhausted after the meeting and had to type out the minutes in a trance-like state. At the end of the meeting day after completing the minutes, I would be totally exhausted. During that period, I restrained from carrying out my physiotherapy, as I was certain I could not cope with the after-effects of the physiotherapy in the presence of immense stress.

As it is also in the nature of autistic individuals to be pedantic, I had to ensure that the minutes were near perfection. I spent a great deal of time and efforts to piece together the jigsaw bits of sentences and words that I had jotted down during the meeting. Perhaps my intuitive intelligence aided me in this aspect because most of the time despite the guesswork, little amendments were made to the minutes by the committee members. It is also with this same intelligence that I have pieced together the answers to the mystery behind *autistic spectrum disorders*. Being the secretary of the meeting had its plus points as it spurred my subsequent promotion and also helped to improve my writing skills. This seemed to be God's plan in teaching me how to rely on His strength day by day, and preparing me for the writing skills that is essential in the exposition of my life experiences and findings.

About this same time, I also managed to pass my driving test after three tries. The most that one could accumulate was 18 demerit points to be able to pass the driving test. Other than demerit points, if you committed a grave error that was considered dangerous, you could get a stamp that said "immediate failure". The first test I managed to scrap twenty four demerit points but with three marks that said "immediate failure". The second test I managed no "immediate failure" but achieved fifty demerit points. My instructor commented that I was perhaps his worst driving student ever. The third test, I committed a grave mistake that could have been deemed an "immediate failure" depending on interpretation but the tester was surprisingly lenient and I managed to pass with eight points.

When I first took driving lessons, I was very unsure whether I could actually drive due to the impairment of my senses. Perhaps, at that point in time, I had recovered sufficiently and my awareness improved enough to allow me to pass my driving test. However, I still attribute my success as being from God as I had never had much confidence that it was something I could achieve.

Anxiety was also a significant disability that could have jeopardised my success. During all three tests I had a problem with parking: the driving test required the completion of parallel and reverse parking, using a car that had a manual gearbox. A manually driven car requires the delicate control and coordination of the clutch and accelerator and any slight mishandling could result in the car engine dieing down. Parking generally requires good coordination of the clutch and accelerator. Because of the excessive anxiety, on all three occasions, I could not seem to control my legs while parking. My legs took on a life of their own. They shook uncontrollably and the car shook rhythmically in the same fashion. The forces applied on the clutch and accelerator by my shaking legs came on-and-off and the car engine responded in kind. It was truly a horrific sight to behold and I was totally embarrassed. On all three occasions, I had to stop the car on its tracks and ashamedly asked the tester to excuse me of my anxiety and give me some time to recuperate.

Even when I passed my driving I would only drive on familiar routes. On unfamiliar routes, I would need someone else in the passenger seat to guide me. On familiar routes, I could already remember all the traffic lights, the turns and other unique road features. With this pattern already inscribed into my memory, I just had to adhere to it to reach my destination. The impairment in my senses did not proof to be much of a disability. However, on unfamiliar routes, not only were traffic lights and other normative road features unfamiliar, I had to also look out for road signs and nearby structures that told me whether I was going on the correct route, as well as unique road features that were specific to the route. With the impairment in my visual senses, I had to make use of other people as my eyes.

One of the greatest regrets in my life was that I was not able to reciprocate when it came to friendships. Towards the end of my Junior College days, I shifted to a new residence. When I shifted to the new residence, I did not inform any of my friends of my new address and telephone number. All my former friends could not contact me and in the throes of the juxtaposition of *autism* and depression, I did not make any effort to keep in touch with them. One of my friends managed to get hold of my office contact in the military staff directory and subsequently kept me in the loop when it came to any outings. I was also included in the email list of those friends that I frequently played basketball with during my Junior College days.

Throughout the course of pathology, I had other "good" friends in that they frequently tried to open up to me or included me in their activities. However, after some time of staid response on my part, these friends naturally disappeared. I really regret how I treated my friends. For example, sometimes I did not turn up for their birthday parties without any reason. Other times, even if I did turn up for their birthday parties, I did not buy any birthday presents or bought inappropriate presents. I definitely did not do my part in showing care and concern to my friends. Neither did I offer any help or advice when they needed it. Moreover, I had little comprehension of the social issues typical of that age as my thoughts were very much confined to my earlier years and restricted to my particular interests.

Nowadays I find it easier to make friends and maintain friendships as I come out of the prison cell defined by *autism*. I can better comprehend people's thoughts and emotions; I can better interpret social cues, facial expressions and body language; I can better interpret common social situations that become the central topics of discussions; my interests have also become more aligned with my peers. With this better understanding of people and events, I am more empathetic towards feelings and able to reciprocate to intentions and emotions.

I have recently just passed the third level of the Chartered Financial Analyst examinations. This is the last level of the examinations but I am not yet able to obtain the charter as I do not have the relevant working experience. I am not certain why I took this course of study in the first place. My girlfriend was doing it, my friends were doing it, and so I decided to give it a try. Perhaps, it could also provide more career options and would stand me in good stead when I finally resolve my autistic tendencies and become more able to decide on my own future. I do not want to be eternally bogged down by my past and hopefully the stones that I have laid in the throes of *autism* provide sufficient foundation for my path into the future. Wish me good luck!

Timeline of my life

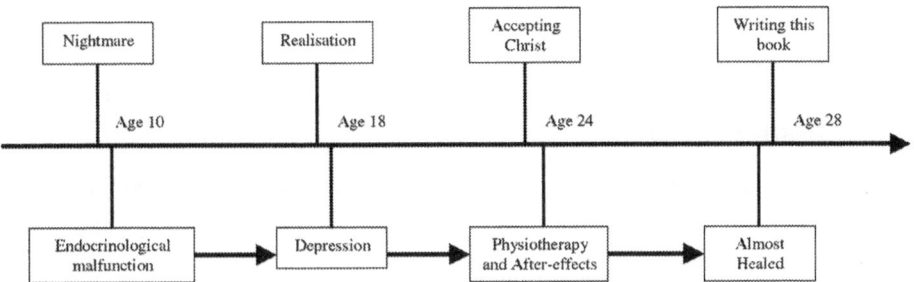

6

The Serotonin Connection

The serotonin system

Serotonin is a neurotransmitter used by brain cells called neurons to signal other neurons. Neurotransmitters act as the medium of communication between neurons in the brain and play a large part in the integrative thinking process of the brain.

Nearly all cell bodies of central serotogenic neurons are located in the dorsal midbrain and brain stem and serotonin is projected in a pervasive fashion throughout the brain as shown in the following figure:

Serotogenic neurons and serotonin projection in central nervous system

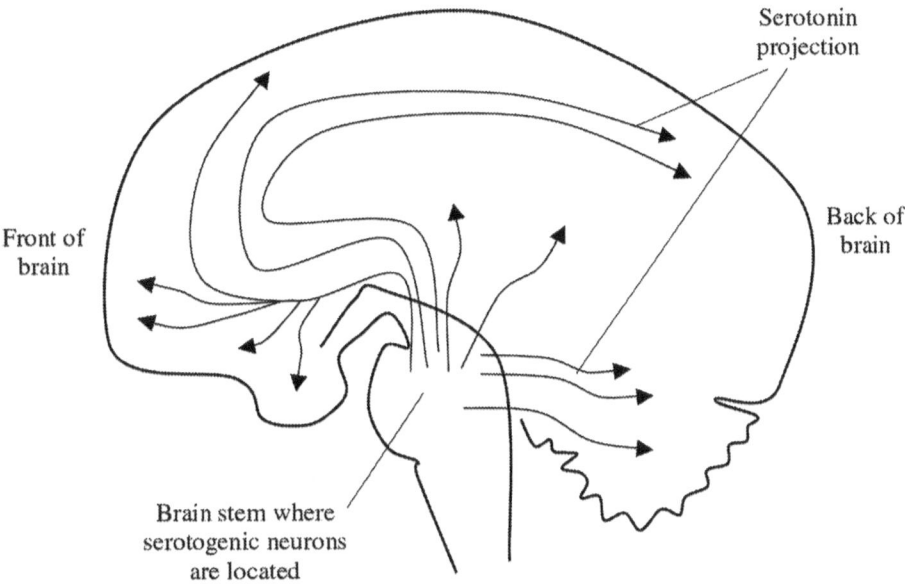

Serotonin is synthesized from tryptophan as follows:

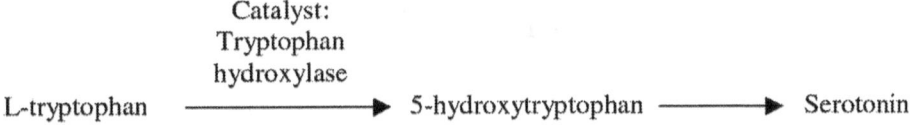

L-tryptophan ⟶ [Catalyst: Tryptophan hydroxylase] ⟶ 5-hydroxytryptophan ⟶ Serotonin

Tryptophan is found in our blood plasma. It is transported into the brain across the blood-brain barrier (BBB) by an active protein shuttle for which five other amino acids also compete. Some studies have indicated that the content of serotonin in the brain is partly dependent on the brain tryptophan levels.[1] If this is true, the amount of tryptophan being transported into the brain through the BBB can affect the brain serotonin levels.

Serotonin dysfunction appears to play an aetiologic role in a very high percentage of diseases, disorders and minor upsets of the human nervous system. Its role is not always straightforward as sometimes com-morbid symptoms seem to indicate both excess and reduced serotonin concurrently. Moreover, people vary tremendously and serotogenic approaches intended to heal these disorders can sometimes work for one person and prove ineffective or have adverse effects for another. Our current understanding of serotonin and how it works is far from complete.

Some clinical behaviours modulated by serotonin

- Mood

- Fear and anxiety

- Learning and memory

- Cognitive control

- Appetite

- Sleep

- Sexual function

- Impulse control

- Developmental behaviour

- Aging and neurodegeneration

- Motivation and reward

- Pain sensitivity

- Emesis

- Mycoclonis

- Neuroendocrine regulation

- Circadian rhythm

- Stress response

- Carcinoid syndrome

Some physiological symptoms of excess serotonin

- Migraine headaches

- Asthma and other allergic reactions

- Insomnia

- Hot flushes

- Edema (swelling)

- Rhinitis

- Sore throat

- Bronchial cough

- Nausea

- Intestinal spasms

- Suppression of immune system

- Contraction of smooth muscles

- Excessive thirst

- Raised blood pressure

- Accelerated heartbeat

- Increased sweating

Serotonin and depression

There is abundant evidence that deficiencies of tryptophan (the pre-cursor of serotonin), serotonin and serotonergic brain activity are rife among depressives. It is a well known fact that anti-depressants that boost serotonin have been particularly effective for the treatment of depression. These anti-depressants boost serotonin levels in the central nervous system by either increasing the precursors to serotonin, catalyzing the synthesis of serotonin from its precursors, or by blocking the reuptake of serotonin by the neurons that release it.

Over the past years, tryptophan depletion has provided another means to examine serotonin systems in depression. Some studies found that tryptophan depletion induces depressive symptom exacerbation in healthy controls at genetic risk for depression and in untreated, remitted patients with a history of depression. Other studies found that tryptophan depletion does not exacerbate these symptoms in control subjects without genetic risk for depression and in untreated symptomatic depressed subjects.[2] This could mean that serotonin levels in the brain are not solely dependent on tryptophan levels. Other factors such as the availability of the catalyst and the sensitivity of the serotonin receptors may also play a role in the serotonin levels.

Serotonin and anxiety

The relationship between serotonin and anxiety is unclear. Some studies have shown that too little serotonin promotes anxiety while others have indicated the opposite. These studies seem to indicate that abnormal levels of serotonin (whether too high or low) can lead to excessive anxiety. Serotonin Reuptake Inhibitors (anti-depressants) have also been found to be useful in the treatment of anxiety disorders.

Serotonin and aggression/violence

There seems to be a link between low serotonin in the brain and impulsive, explosive acts of violence.[3] It occurs uniformly in mice and men, in feisty chickens and scrappy alcoholics, in children who torture their pets and parents who massacre their children.[4]

Serotonin and repetitive behaviour

Serotonin Reuptake Inhibitors have also been found to be effective in the treatment of patients with Obsessive Compulsive Disorder (OCD). It lessens their compulsive thoughts and actions, and reduces repetitive behaviour.

Serotonin and memory/learning

Cognitive performance, particularly impairments in memory and learning have been found to be associated with serotonin dysfunction.[5]

Serotonin and autism

Studies have indicated that serotonin may be implicated in autistic disorders. In 1961, Schain and Freedman reported elevation of whole blood serotonin in patients with *autism*.[6] Subsequent studies have also confirmed that about one quarter[7] to one third[8] of individuals with *autism* have elevated levels of whole blood serotonin. These findings remain inconclusive as they are reported only in the minority of autistic individuals. There seems to be some contradictions between high levels of serotonin in the blood and some of the symptoms of autistic disorders that point towards low levels of serotonin in the central nervous system.

Furthermore, research has shown that medications that act to increase serotonin or serotonergic activity seem to alleviate some of the effects of *autism*. Some antidepressants have been shown to reduce the ritualistic behaviour and aggression in more than 50 percent of children and adults with *autism* in various trials.[9] In a large survey, one biomedical treatment received the most praise from parents of autistic children: megadoses of two nutrients that are required for serotonin synthesis, vitamin B6 and magnesium.[10] Parents' favourable reviews outnumbered bad ones by ten to one. These positive findings have also been replicated in over a dozen other clinical trials.[11]

Further evidence of serotonin involvement in *autism* comes from a pharmacological study by depleting tryptophan, the pre-cursor to serotonin. Exacerbation of anxiety and ritualistic behaviours such as whirling, flapping, pacing and banging, etc occurred in more than 50 percent of adults with *autism* after tryptophan depletion.[12] One study postulated that their penchant for repeated movements could be an instinctive attempt at serotogenic self-medication.[13]

It has been found that the values for overall serotonin synthesis in the brains of autistic patients are significantly different. One study reported that in non-autistic children, the values of whole-brain serotonin synthesis change during development, such that the values for children aged between 3 to 8 years old are three times higher than those measured in adults. In autistic children aged between 3 to 8 years old, whole-brain serotonin synthesis values were only slightly (one time) higher than adult values.

These observations suggest that excessive production of serotonin outside the brain (as evident from high blood plasma levels) could be promoting a deficiency within the brain (as evident from reduced synthesis and the favourable effects of antidepressants).

Serotonin and PTSD

Studies have found that inescapably shocked animals develop decreased central nervous system serotonin levels.[14] This indicates that severe trauma may also result in reduced serotonin synthesis in the central nervous system.

Serotonin reuptake inhibitors (SSRI) have also been found to be effective in the treatment of chronic PTSD.[15] In some studies, fluoxetine (Prozac) was found to have a positive effect on the dimensions of affect dysregulation, distorted relationships with others and loss of sustaining beliefs. The increased availability of serotonin in the hippocampus may also activate inhibitory pathways in the limbic system that prevent the initiation of habitual emergency responses.[16] Some parallels can be drawn between the efficacy of SSRIs for the treatment of both the chronic effects of PTSD and for *autism*.

Serotonin and mental retardation

Serotonin is critically involved in guiding neurodevelopment during the early stages of life. Serotonin and its associated transporters and receptors are found very early in development (by 4 months of gestation in humans). Serotonin appears to have critical effects on neurogenesis, morphogenesis and synaptogenesis in the developing brain.

Serotonin may have a role in the developmental neuropathological abnormalities found in the hippocampus, amygdala, and cerebellum in autistic disorder.[17] These abnormalities may lead to mental retardation.

The serotonin connection

When I first discovered the physiotherapy that could help to diminish the effects off my affliction, I did not yet know the classification of the disorder. While some of the symptoms were similar to those of *autism* and *asperger's syndrome*, the prevalent perception was that these were childhood disorders and that with my normal childhood, it was not probable that I was suffering from these disorders. On the other hand, PTSD seemed even more improbable as I did not experience any of the classical traumatic experiences that were in line with the definition of PTSD. There was also little study on the enduring physiological effects of PTSD that many others are suffering from.

When I carried out the physiotherapy, some of the physical symptoms that included migraine headaches, eczema and gastro-intestinal disturbances resurfaced. It reminded me of the period after the nightmare episode when I had the same symptoms. A few years after I started carrying out the physiotherapy, I chanced upon some literature describing the physical effects of an overdose of serotonin which could come from natural foods, medicines such as antidepressants or negative ions. These physical effects were the same as those that were exacerbated by my physiotherapy. I became convinced that my illness was the result of too much serotonin being supplied from the afflicted area which was the focal point of my physiotherapy.

Subsequently, I came across some literature on the inconclusive findings of high levels of whole-blood serotonin in autistic individuals. One study found that about one-third of autistic individuals had high levels of whole-blood serotonin. Even though these studies were inconclusive, I became pretty certain that I was suffering from an illness that has some relation to *autism*. I rationalized that the inconclusive findings could be due to serotonin being produced by two separate systems: the endocrine system and the central nervous system. For those autistic individuals where whole-blood levels appeared normal, the central nervous system could have modulated its production to normalize the levels of whole-blood serotonin. This may also explain the conflicting symptoms of *autism* that point towards both excess serotonin (hypomania, hyperactivity, etc) and reduced serotonin (depression, anxiety, aggression, repetitive behaviour, etc). The change in production in both the endocrine system and central nervous system could affect the dispersion of serotonin in the central nervous system.

As I read through DSM-IV-TR, I became even more convinced that *autism*, *childhood disintegrative disorder* and *asperger's syndrome* all lie on the same spectrum of disorders. As my illness is also on this same spectrum, I realized that the spectrum did not only comprise of disorders generalized by onset during childhood and that there was another part of the spectrum characterized by onset during later stages of life and that was not currently clearly specified.

Remembering that my physical symptoms had set in after the nightmare episode, I deduced that the nightmare episode must be the cause of this endocrinological malfunction. I then came across some literature on the chronic
physiological symptoms of PTSD that included somatic complaints, emotional detachment and social estrangement. I could clearly see that there were
parallels between these symptoms and those of *autism* and *asperger's syndrome*.

If the chronic physiological effects of PTSD and *pervasive development disorders* (*autism* and *asperger's syndrome*) all lie on the same spectrum of disorders
depending on the age of onset, then it is reasonable to deduce that they are of
the same aetiology and that *pervasive development disorders* are also caused by
acute trauma. We can logically assume that the main differences between the
symptoms of pervasive development disorders and the chronic physiological
symptoms of PTSD are due to onset at different ages and the differential
effect on the person's cognitive, language and behavioural development. Furthermore, in the same way as congenital thyroid disorders can cause mental
retardation, mental retardation is also more common in *autism* as compared to
asperger's syndrome because of the earlier onset in the former, whereas PTSD is
not usually associated with mental retardation.

Depending on the genetic make-up of the person, and the nature and extent
of the trauma, this serotogenic malfunction may occur in the face of trauma.
This serotogenic malfunction is more likely to occur if the victim is male. The
serotogenic malfunction could be the body's natural defence or some form of
protective device against the stressful effects of the acute trauma on the central
nervous system (acting in some ways similar to the airbag of a car). It is not the
only endocrinological defence but part of a wide array of endocrinological
responses to the acute trauma. It is however perhaps the most permanent and
most troublesome physiological response related to the trauma. This endocrinological malfunction seems to make the victim more alert to "danger" by
inducing hypersensitivity and hyperactivity. On the other hand, it may
dampen the psychological effects of the trauma by playing an important role in
the dissociative amnesia of the traumatic event. Perhaps if the endocrinological defence does not kick in or provides an inadequate defence, the trauma
may cause permanent psychological effects related to the shattering of the person's identity. This may come across as personality disorders such as borderline personality disorders and multiple personality disorders. It may also
explain why females are more susceptible to both these two types of disorders.

If trauma is indeed the cause of *pervasive development disorders*, we should move away from the current narrow view of PTSD where trauma is defined by exposure to an event which involved actual or threatened death or serious injury, or a threat to the physical integrity of self or others. We should widen the scope to include any trauma that is significant enough to cause either the intrusive or constrictive symptoms of PTSD.

Because *autism* begins at a very early age, the onset of the serotogenic malfunction could be pre-natal, peri-natal or during infancy. This means that even foetuses and infants can be subject to acute trauma. The nature of the acute trauma is probably very different for infants and its severity is more likely imagined rather than a true reflection of actual events. Trauma for foetuses is even less easily understood. Perhaps thoughts of abortion by the mother may induce acute stress in the foetus. Trauma experienced by the mother may also induce the serotogenic malfunction in the foetus.

Some studies have concluded that the incidents of *autism* and *asperger's syndrome* have risen over the years. This could be because of the increased stress in our society, the widespread media and the trend of the media to depict horror and violence. Abortion is also on a rising trend and mere talk of abortion may induce acute stress in the foetus. Child abuse is also more rampant and prevalent. Prevention of *autism* and *asperger's syndrome* would thus be by the avoidance of any trauma to the expectant mother, the foetus or the infant. Infants should be given constant re-assurance that the parental figure is nearby and avoid any exposure to horror and violent films. Expectant mothers should reduce their risk of any traumatic experience and avoid watching any horror and violent films. Care should be taken when abortion is being considered and contemplated. Parents should shower their children with love rather than perform acts of hatred on them.

The serotonin dispersion

Initially upon onset of the serotogenic malfunction during the traumatic experience, the serotonin produced within the endocrine system will shoot up to its peak. This intensely excess serotonin from the endocrine system will invoke a response from the central nervous system in its attempt to regulate and moderate overall serotonin levels. In doing so, the central nervous system will significantly reduce its production (the mechanism of which is not yet understood). This may lead to uneven dispersion of serotonin in the central nervous system where there is excess serotonin near the blood-brain barrier and reduced serotonin in areas of the brain further from this interface. The immediate effect of excess serotonin near the blood-brain barrier will be mania and hyperarousal. The immediate effect of the reduced serotonin further from the brain-blood interface could be delirium, lack of clarity and memory loss of the traumatic event.

Overtime, the serotonin produced by the endocrine system will diminish but in some individuals (especially males), this serotonin production does not diminish to its normal levels. The remaining abnormal production results in a chronic array of symptoms precipitated by the excess serotonin from the endocrine system. The production of serotonin within the central nervous system will respond and adapt to the permanent changes of serotonin from the endocrine system in its bid to achieve an unnatural state of equilibrium. In other words, the central nervous system will reduce its serotonin production. This is supported by findings in studies that there is a reduction in the ratio of TRP/LNAA in *autistic disorder*. This means that there is decreased tryptophan transport across the blood-brain barrier and subsequently decreased serotonin synthesis.[18] Where both these effects cancel each other out, overall levels of excess serotonin may not be detected and that could explain why high levels of whole-blood serotonin are not detected in a large percentage of individuals with *autism*. Concurrent depression may also negate the effects of increased production of serotonin within the endocrine system, resulting in normal detected levels of whole-blood serotonin.

No consistent pattern between symptoms of *autism* and elevated whole blood serotonin has emerged. This supports the postulation that the symptoms of autism are independent of the aggregate levels of whole blood serotonin but dependent on the dispersion of serotonin in the central nervous system.

The dispersion of serotonin within the central nervous system varies for different individuals depending on sex, genetic make-up and the extent of the endocrinological malfunction. That could explain why there are conflicting symptoms for different individuals suffering from the same disorder. For example, some individuals may have a heightened sexual interest while others may have reduced libido. A small minority may have special analytical or memory abilities, for example where complex sums can be mentally calculated, or the words on one page of a book can be memorized visually and with great accuracy.

There seems to be some differences in sexes. Females with *autism* seem to use more visualization of images in their thought processes. From my personal experience, I use very little visualization of images in my thought processes and that could be because of my gender.

Serotogenic inflammation

The increased serotonin secretion could be due to the inflammation of serotonergic neurons that are thought to be located at the genitals. This may also explain why *autism* is about four times more prevalent among males than females. It may also explain why there is an unusually high incidence of surgery to the genitals of children with *asperger's syndrome*, most often correction of a phimosis or orchidopexy for maldescended testicle.

Other than secretion of serotonin, there may also be secretion of other neurotransmitters such as GABA and acetylcholine, etc, some of which may also contribute to the various symptomatic features of autism. There may also be changes in levels of testosterone and opoid peptides (e.g. endorphin).

Secondary effects–opoid peptides

Why do people get "butterflies" in the stomach when they are anxious? Why do antidepressant drugs cause nausea or abdominal upsets in many who use them? The reason is that humans have two brains–one in the skull and one in the gut. The gut's brain is known as the enteric nervous system. It appears that the increased endocrine serotonin in *autism* also has adverse effects on the enteric nervous system. Food is broken down to amino acids via intermediate compounds known as peptides in the gut. The excess serotonin affects the breaking down of food and results in excess peptides being produced and introduced into the blood stream and subsequently into the brain. The peptides bind with the opoids in the brain to form opoid-peptides (endorphins).

Excess opoid-peptides may result in some of the symptoms of the *autistic spectrum disorder*, as follows:

- A "high" similar to that of an adrenaline rush

- Lack of 'normal' motivation

- Little desire for social interactions

- Decreased sensitivity to pain

Diagram of Central Nervous System (CNS)

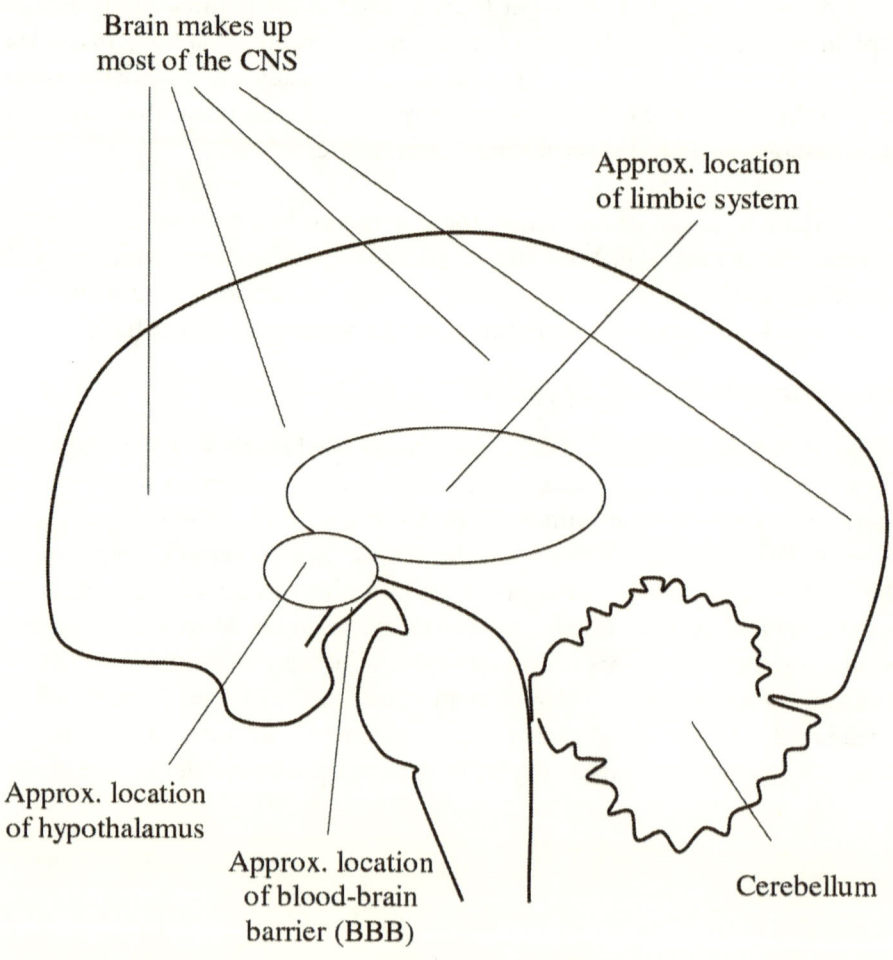

Possible Hypothesis—Serotogenic dispersion in autistic spectrum disorders and related symptoms

Item	Region	Function	Proximity from blood-brain barrier (BBB)	Serotogenic Dysfunction	Related Symptoms*
1.	Hypothalamus	Respond "automatically" to chemical stimuli of the body. Connects the central nervous system to the endocrine system. Communicate sensations felt in the endocrine system to the central nervous system. Controls sexual urges.	Beside BBB.	Increased serotonin from BBB outweighs decreased serotonin from CNS.	Hypersensitivity. Heightened sexual interest. Hyperactivity.
2.	Limbic system	In charge of memory, emotions, attention and learning. Regulate instinctive behaviour. Some areas of the limbic system are associated with anger, anxiety, excitement and sexual interest.	Further from BBB.	Decreased serotonin from CNS outweighs increased serotonin from BBB.	Emotional apathy and social impairment. Learning disability and memory impairment. Deficit in attention. Increased anxiety, aggression and ritualistic behaviour. Reduced sexual interest.

Item	Region	Function	Proximity from blood-brain barrier (BBB)	Serotogenic Dysfunction	Related Symptoms*
3.	Brain	Main mass of the encephalon. Elaborates and compares information internal and external to the body; transforms them into sensations, and stores them as memories. All processes that affect the elaboration of thoughts, decision making, motor or endocrine reaction of the body, takes place here.	Far from BBB.	Decreased serotonin from CNS outweighs increased serotonin from BBB.	Impairment of senses and sensory integration. Learning disability and memory impairment. Impairs verbal skills. Impairs relation and integration of experiences.
4.	Cerebellum	Modulates the movements of the body.	Far from BBB.	Decreased serotonin from CNS outweighs increased serotonin from BBB.	Poor motor coordination skills.

*   Some symptoms may be associated with changes in levels of testosterone and
     opoid peptides (e.g. endorphin).

Important Points to Remember

- The *autistic spectrum disorder* is caused by a permanent serotogenic malfunction in the endocrine system that produces unwanted serotonin.

- The serotogenic malfunction in the endocrine system affects the serotonin synthesis in the central nervous system.

- The combination of these two effects results in asymmetrical serotonin dispersion in the central nervous system.

- The asymmetrical serotonin dispersion leads to the varying symptoms of the *autistic spectrum disorder*.

- Excess serotonin may also result in increased levels of opoid-peptides and this may contribute to some of the symptoms of *autistic spectrum disorder*.

7

The Miracle Cure

The inflammation of the serotogenic neurons[1] occurs at the junction where the crown of the glans, cavernous body and spongy body of the penis intersects. The locations are illustrated in the following diagram of the anatomy:

---

1. Please note that this is based on a conjecture. The mechanism may be different but nonetheless the physiotherapy will still work.

a.   *Plan view of anatomy from bottom*

b.   *Cross-sectional view of anatomy from front*

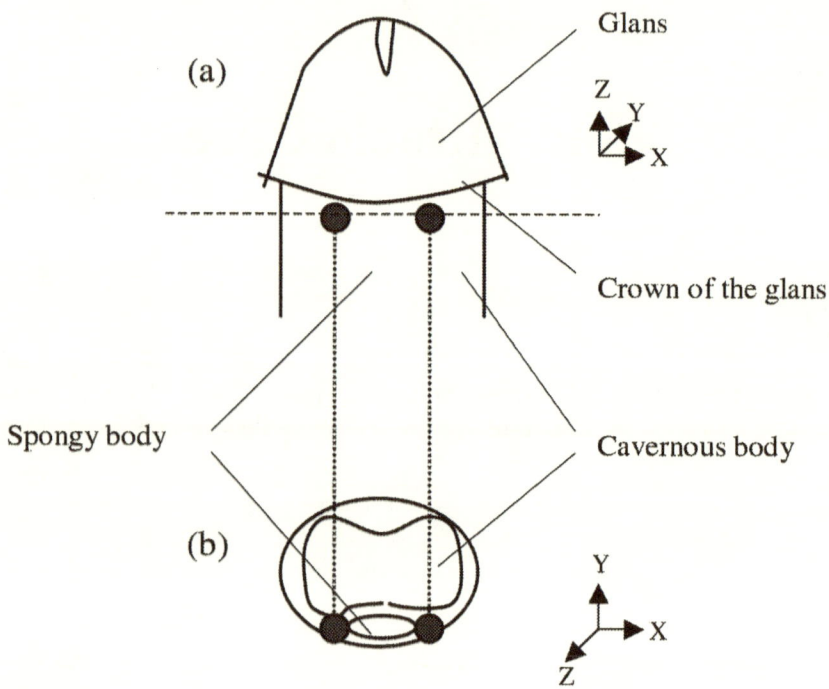

● Denotes afflicted area

This area although small is the main culprit of hyperserotonemia and *autism* for males. It is hypothesized that there is a similar area for females. The area for males and females is probably the same prior to foetal formation of the organs, when the sex of the foetus has yet to be determined. This area will evolve differently in subjects of different sex in line with the formation of the genital organs. Its origination from the genitals may explain the gender differences in the prevalence of the disorder in the different sexes.

Physiotherapy is conducted by applying force to this area. To carry this out, first clamp the afflicted area between the index finger and the thumb. The tip of the index finger is then used to apply force to the area. This is illustrated in the diagrams as follows:

Step 1
Diagram of penis being twisted so that afflicted area faces upwards

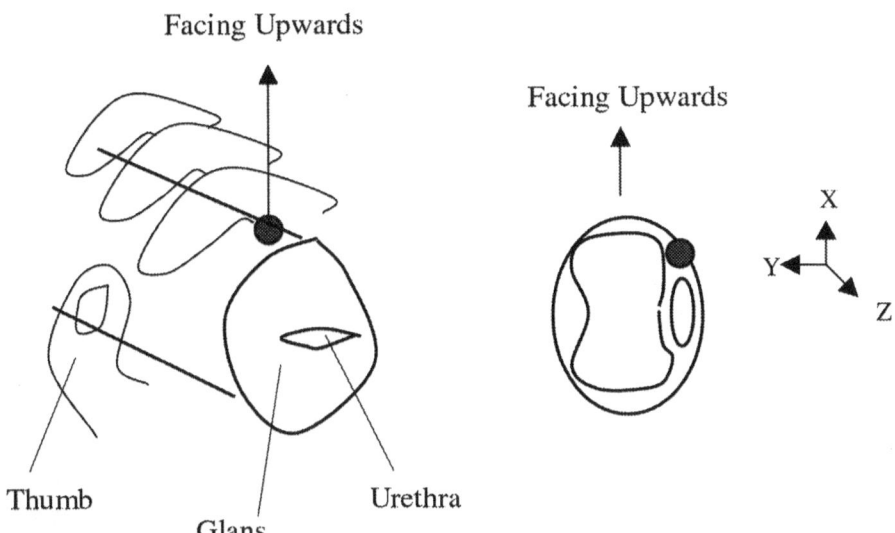

Step 2
Diagram of hand holding penis to provide support

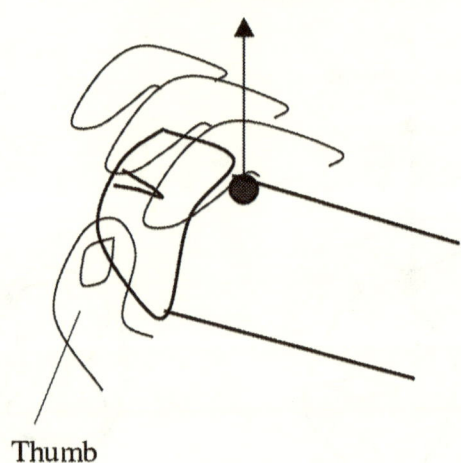

Facing Upwards

Thumb

Step 3
Diagram of index finger applying pressure (side view)

The index finger of the other hand applying
force on afflicted area by clamping area
between index finger and thumb

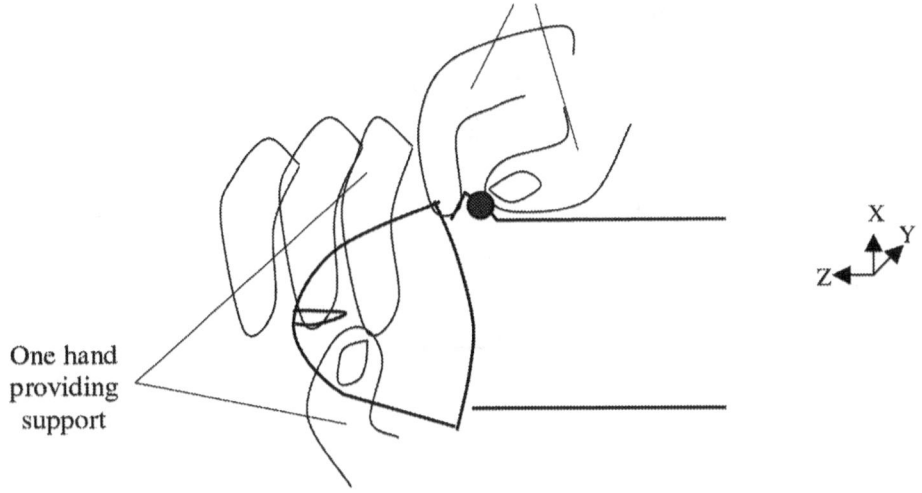

X
Y
Z

One hand
providing
support

Step 4
Diagram of forces (side view)

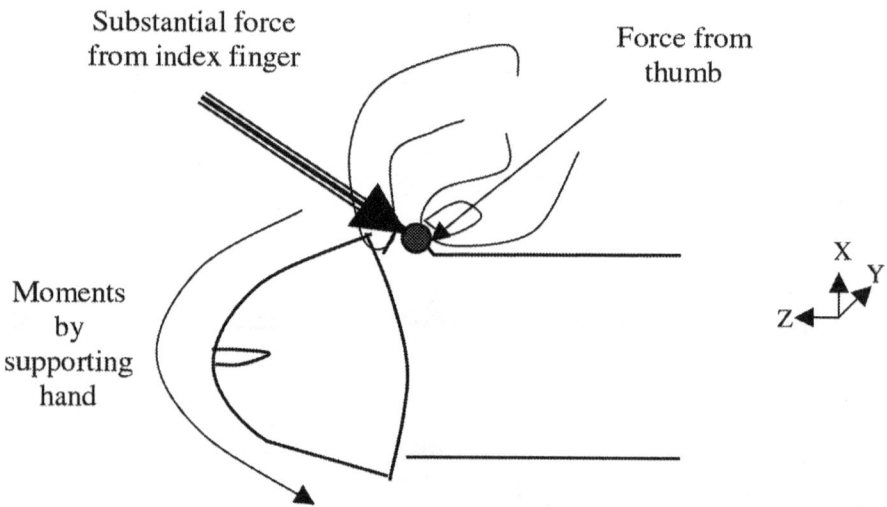

Substantial force
from index finger

Force from
thumb

Moments
by
supporting
hand

It is of utmost importance that force is applied generously. It is also vital that a sequence is followed that includes masturbation. Masturbation should first be carried out to increase the blood flow in the cavernous and spongy bodies of the penis. The afflicted neurons will then be compelled into a small area. Immediately upon ejaculation, force should be generously applied to the afflicted area. This cycle should be repeated with the more times the merrier. The more this cycle is adhered to, the more effective is the treatment.

Force should not be applied during erection and prior to ejaculation. The physiotherapy will prove ineffective in such a case as the hardened cavernous and spongy bodies of the penis will form a protective barrier to the afflicted area.

Force should not be applied long after ejaculation as blood would have vacated the cavernous and spongy bodies of the penis and the soft backing to the afflicted area would absorb most of the force being applied and would very much diminish its effectiveness.

It should be noted that complete improvement in the condition will not be immediate and will be gradual. A word of caution is that the physiotherapy will be followed by a period of symptomatic after-effects that will last for close to a year.

As I am uncertain of the long-lasting effects of this therapy, readers should try the therapy at their own risk.

Castration

If the origination of the autistic spectrum disorder is from the genitals, we can intuitively conceive that castration would be effective in treating the disorder. This is however too drastic an action as there are too many other implications that could include both psychological and hormonal effects. The penis plays an important role in the definition of one's identity, and is an important arte-fact that defines a person's purposes, roles and functions associated with his gender. Perhaps this can be best illustrated by transsexuals who go for a sex change operation to acquire a pseudo phallus. Hormonal changes would also occur with the deficiency in testosterone. The price of castration is indeed too high a price to pay to cure the effects of the *autistic spectrum disorder*.

The Cure of the Future

Without doubt, science will find an improved cure for the *autistic spectrum disorder*. The cure could be by surgical means with the surgical removal of the afflicted area; it could be by some form of radiation therapy to destroy the cells that are malfunctioning, or it could be an improved form of the physiotherapy using a better technique or with the help of other aids.

The After-Effect

During the period immediately following the physiotherapy, transitional symptomatic after-effects are encountered. These after-effects are associated with the sudden decline in serotonin injection from the endocrine system. The central nervous system notices this decline, boosts its own serotonin synthesis extravagantly and in an unstable fashion, resulting in mania and other physical symptoms associated with the fluctuations in serotonin.

Plot of serotonin production versus time before and after physiotherapy

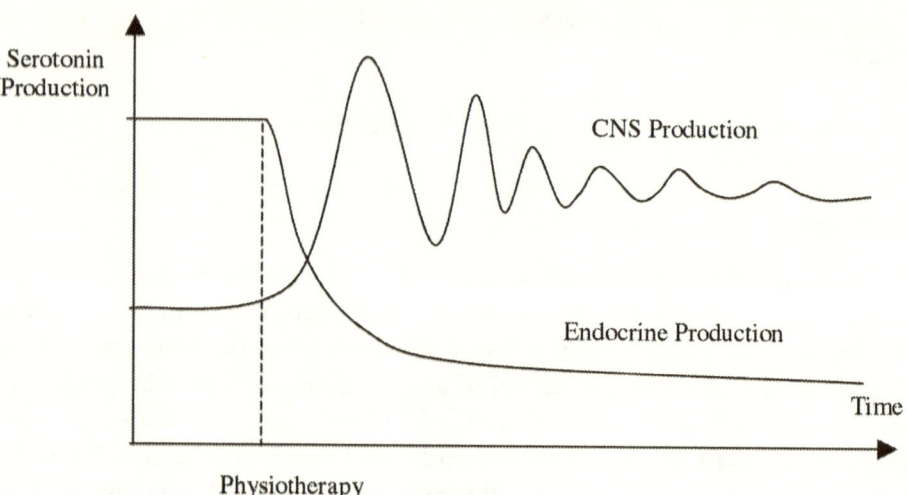

During the period of transient fluctuations in serotonin, certain symptomatic after-effects will be encountered, as follows:

- First phase of hypomania bordering on mania;

- Subsequent phase of subsiding hypomania, intertwining with depression;

The physiological after-effects include the following:

- Migraine headaches

- Increased frequency of breaking wind

- Bloated stomach

- Loosening of muscles (jumping muscles)

- Eczema

- Gastro-Intestinal problems

- Memory impairment

- Suppressed immune system

8

Parallels with Hyperthyroidism

For a better understanding of the *autistic spectrum disorder* (ASD), parallels can be drawn between ASD and Hyperthyroidism. While it is evident that Hyperthyroidism is usually caused by a thyroid malfunction, the aetiology of ASD is not yet understood. By comparing these two disorders, we can draw some insights into the prevalence and aetiology of ASD and perhaps infer that ASD may also be caused by a neuro-endocrinological malfunction and not merely by a neurological malfunction as previously conceived.

Thyroid imbalances are not always easily detected. It is only recently that the medical fraternity has come to the realisation that minimal thyroid imbalances have an important effect on mental and physical health. There are still many people whose thyroid conditions remain undiagnosed. Many psychiatrists focus on the psychological causes and do not perform physical examinations to detect the physical causes for mental symptoms.[1] One study showed that when psychiatrists use conventional psychiatric criteria to assess hyperthyroid patients, they diagnose nearly half of the patients as depressed or suffering from an anxiety disorder.[2]

In the same way, if ASD is indeed a neuro-endocrinological condition as postulated, there are probably many people with ASD but where its effects could be minimal and where the impairment not severe enough to be diagnosed as a psychiatric condition. These subtle neuro-endocrinological differences may also result in secondary psychiatric conditions such as depression and anxiety disorders that mask the primary imbalances. These patients will be diagnosed with these other psychiatric conditions. ASD could in effect be much more widespread than we are currently aware.

Many people experiencing fatigue, lack of interest in life, and an inability to function as they once did, suffer for years. Other people may feel detached in all aspects of life including emotionally, sensually and socially, and they are pessimistic and have little hope about their future. Deep down, these people know that there is something not quite right about themselves but in their struggle to appear normal to the people around them, these people adjust and conceal their difficulties and continue to work and take care of responsibilities at home. These people may not seek help or treatment for their symptoms. These people may be suffering from a neuro-endocrinological condition such as thyroid malfunction or ASD.

Some of their reluctance to seek medical advice stems from the stigma our culture puts on mental disorders. Mental conditions are viewed by many with contempt and derision. Many sufferers do not seek treatment because they fear ridicule from friends and relatives. There are others who fear being discriminated against by prospective employers if they have a history of being diagnosed with a psychiatric illness.

Dr. Robert Graves was the first to provide the classic description of what is now known as the Graves' disease (one possible cause of thyroid malfunction). In his description of this "newly observed affection of the thyroid gland in females,"[3] he highlighted symptoms of the nervous system and used the term *globus hystericus* because of the many psychiatric manifestations exhibited by his patients. Dr. Caleb Parry, who had recognised the condition before Graves but expired before his observations were published, wrote: "In more than one of these [patients], the affliction of the head has amounted almost to madness."[4] For decades, in fact, Graves' disease was considered to be a mental illness rather than a true thyroid disorder. In the same way, ASD may currently be misconstrued as a mental illness because of the lack of knowledge of its endocrinological origin. In years to come, ASD may be regarded as a neuro-endocrinological condition similar in nature to a thyroid disorder, and not purely just a mental illness.

In time to come, when we fully understand the aetiology of ASD and when the chemical imbalances can be arrested early, the mystery behind ASD will be unveiled and our perception of its severity will correspondingly diminish.

Mental stress seems to trigger and worsen thyroid disease. The early label of "crystallised fright" for thyroid disorder illustrates that this condition was seen as some kind of mental illness that follows a psychological trauma. Research has shown that under stress, the brain emits chemical messages that trigger major responses of the endocrine system. One such response is the overproduction of the stress hormone cortisol by the adrenal glands. Repeated overproduction of this hormone and other chemicals results in many of the deleterious effects associated with stress.[5] If you handle stress well, the response of the endocrine system is minimal and short-lived. If you experience stress for a long time or have difficulty coping with the stress, your endocrine system may go awry and cause chronic health problems.

The likely outcome and permanence of any endocrinological changes as a result of stress would thus be dependent on the nature of the stress and the genetic make-up of the person that is being subject to the stress. While chronic stress could induce a thyroid malfunction, acute trauma that invokes a perceptual change of the safety of this world and the fundamental fabric of a person's support system could cause both a thyroid malfunction and/or the endocrinological malfunction related to ASD. There are also gender differences for both these neuro-endocrinological disorders. While thyroid disorder is more commonly associated with females, ASD is more commonly associated with males. Genetic make-up and hereditary factors can also predispose a person to a higher or lower possibility of being afflicted with either of the two disorders.

The mental effects of Hyperthyroidism are somewhat similar to that of ASD. Some hyperthyroid people experience hypomania and hyperactivity. They feel infused with energy, optimism and self-confidence. Some compare the feeling to the analogy of being high on potent mind-altering drugs. The speedy mind becomes compromised by loss of memory. There may also be impaired cognition and irrational behaviour. ASD is also often characterised by hyperactivity. In my own experience of ASD, both hyperactivity and hypomania were present.

Hyperthyroid people often become easily irritated and angry. Some may even exhibit uncontrolled aggression and violence. In the same way, some people with *autism, asperger's syndrome* and *post traumatic stress disorder* have been known to exhibit aggression and violence that is otherwise uncharacteristic of their persona.

One of the most common mental effects of Hyperthyroidism is anxiety. Likewise, heightened levels of anxiety are commonly associated with both *autism* and *asperger's syndrome*. Some sufferers of *post traumatic stress disorder* also exhibit abnormal levels of anxiety even many years after the occurrence of the traumatic event.

In many cases of thyroid malfunction, there is the existence of com-morbid disorders such as depression and of a lesser degree, manic-depression. On many occasions, these disorders develop only as a secondary effect of the thyroid condition. Conventional antidepressants do not help to alleviate the depression if the underlying thyroid imbalance is not corrected. Research has shown that 52 percent of patients who suffer from major depression and do not respond to antidepressants have hypothyroidism.[6] However, upon thyroid hormone treatment being added to the antidepressant, the depression often resolves.

The different forms of ASD are also frequently associated with chronic depression. The depression does not go away even when treated with antidepressants. This could be because both thyroid malfunction and ASD have something in common, that is, they are both neuro-endocrinological conditions. Depression is a neurological condition caused by a malfunction in the detection, regulation and consequently production of neurotransmitters such as serotonin in the brain. Under normal circumstances, when brain serotonin drops to a low level, this will be detected by the brain and the brain will step up its production to bring the serotonin to normal levels. Depression is the consequence of a malfunction in this regulatory system. When an endocrinological condition such as thyroid malfunction or ASD occurs, external hormones or neurotransmitters are being introduced into the brain from the endocrine system. These external chemicals confuse and disrupt the regulatory system and leads to it being unable to distinguish and establish its natural equilibrium.

Hyperthyroidism also has an effect on a person's libido and sex life. The effect of Hyperthyroidism on libido is complex and varied. Hyperthyroidism may result in more or less interest in sex. Some hyperthyroid people who are overwhelmed by their chaotic thoughts and emotional indifference may lose interest in sex. Other hyperthyroid people being in a state of hypomania may find their sex drive increased, and they may become obsessed with sexual thoughts. There is currently little study on the effects of ASD on a person's libido. Some patients diagnosed with *schizoid personality disorder* have been found to display a lack of sexual interest. My own struggles with ASD bespoke of hypomania, which included a heightened sexual interest.

Emotional withdrawal, which is the hallmark of ASD, is also apparent in some cases of Hyperthyroidism.

In summary, the following are the shared mental effects commonly found in both Hyperthyroidism and ASD:

- Hypomania or hyperactivity
- Loss of memory
- Anxiety
- Depression
- Excessive concerns about physical symptoms, real or imaginary
- Emotional withdrawal
- Disorganised thinking
- Aggression

Hyperthyroidism and ASD share many common mental effects and there may be similarities in their aetiology. Thyroid hormone in the brain has the ability to enhance the production of serotonin in brain cells. Excess thyroid hormone may thus lead to the overproduction of serotonin. Imbalances in serotonin could be the key to understanding the shared effects of Hyperthyroidism and ASD. If the increased production of serotonin is responsible for these symptoms in Hyperthyroidism, it can be postulated that the symptoms of ASD are also caused by a similar increase in serotonin in certain parts of the central nervous system.

The development of brain structures in the critical period of rapid growth during the foetal stage and immediately following birth also depends on normal thyroid levels.[7] Infants with congenital hypothyroidism suffer severe neurological problems and mental impairment. In the same way, ASD that occurs at a young age can also lead to central nervous system abnormalities and mental retardation.

Similarities between Hyperthyroidism (HT) and ASD

- HT and ASD are neuro-endocrinological conditions.

- HT and ASD commonly appear to be other forms of psychiatric illnesses and are frequently misdiagnosed.

- HT and ASD are more rampant than currently conceived.

- HT was historically perceived as a mental disorder. In recent times, it is better recognized as a physical disorder. ASD which is currently perceived as a mental disorder may in future be recognised as a physical disorder.

- HT appears to be stress-related. ASD appears to be caused by acute trauma.

- Some of the mental effects of HT and ASD are similar.

- Onset of HT and ASD during early infantile development usually results in central nervous system abnormalities and mental impairment.

9

Dedications to God

This book cannot be complete without a dedication to God. In fact, it would not even have come to print without God's revelations and guidance. Up till now, my whole life story and experiences seem to be carefully planned for one purpose, which is to bring to light the truth behind *autism, asperger's syndrome* and *chronic PTSD*, and in so doing, testify and bring glory to God's name. There is finally hope for those many who suffer from the *autistic spectrum disorder* and greater hope for those who read my testimony and come to accept Jesus Christ as His personal savior.

A few years ago, not having fashioned the physiotherapy to be effective, I was still lingering in the throes of the serotogenic malfunction characteristic of *autistic spectrum disorder*. During that time, I kept on asking God why He did not heal me immediately as He has done for so many people on so many different occasions. Miracles from God have been aplenty both as recorded in the Bible and as experienced in real life: the blind can see and the disabled can walk, but He did not heal me. Was it for some reason that he chose not to heal me immediately?

Even though God did not heal me immediately, He did eventually do so. Sometimes patience is necessary when we do not initially understand God's intention. We have to trust God and continue to abide by Him, and He will not let us down. Even if God does not seem to answer your prayers immediately, it could be because the time is not yet ripe or He has an even higher purpose to fulfill in allowing the problem to prolong. We can only guess at His purposes and cannot fully comprehend them until they come to pass.

The fact that I have pieced together and made clear obscure areas of psychiatry is not due to my own intelligence. It is God's revelations and guidance that has brought about this significant discovery. From the very moment I discovered the physiotherapy to relating my disorder to *autism, asperger's syndrome* and *PTSD*, God has guided me every step of the way.

God's work in me would have begun long ago from the moment I was born. He already knew me even before I was conceived and still in my mother's womb. He already had a pre-destined plan for me right from my birth. Sometimes God's plan may not work out if we do not abide by Him. It is because of the "free will" He allows in us that His plans may go awry. Both Adam and Eve did not abide by God and that led to the birth of sin. Thus my story began when I was born. A new chapter began when I believed and accepted His only begotten Son—Jesus Christ, as my personal savior.

Life may be full of coincidences. I do not believe though that coincidences led me to know God and to me unearthing this significant discovery. The first miracle that occurred was the discovery of the physiotherapy. It was through trial and error with hardly any leads and there was very little initial hope that it would be successful. The second miracle is the circumstances through which I got to know Jesus Christ. My mother prayed for my deliverance and God used her friends to bring her and me to know Christ. The third miracle is relating my disorder to *autism, asperger's syndrome* and *chronic PTSD*. Even though I did not actively research into these disorders, somehow I happened to chance upon literature that revealed to me that I was suffering from these disorders and that they may be related to one another. The fourth miracle is that God surrounded me with many sufferers of thyroid disorder and *asperger's syndrome* from whom I gathered some insights into these disorders.

One thing that strikes me is that on both occasions when God spoke to me through prophetic means, he revealed to me (through other people) that I was intelligent. The second speaking seemed to validate the first. Perhaps God wanted to tell me that my gift is intelligence and He would use it for His purposes.

The following are some of the questions that I have asked both before and after I came to know Christ. I hope that the answers I have gathered and seriously considered will lead and convince you to accept Jesus Christ as your personal savior.

Is there God?

This question has been discussed and debated for years by many philosophers and scientists. I have listed some of the evidences that point towards there being an omnipotent entity.

Our creation has been debated for many years. Creation can only be explained by there being a God or as a result of scientific coincidence. Could it be by coincidence that the "big bang" had resulted in the formation of the Universe and our subsequent evolution from single-celled organisms, or could it be that God created the Universe? Both the "big bang theory" and "evolutionary theory" remain unproven and remain at best scientific postulations. The creation of the Universe by God appears more likely when taking into account other evidences that cannot otherwise be scientifically explained.

One of the most convincing evidences that there is a God is that of "conscience" and "guilt". In many societies and cultures, there appears to be a common denominator of what is considered righteous. Righteousness has even been formalized into the laws of man. If we do not abide by our conscience, we will feel guilt. Guilt is what keeps us in check and enables us to abide by our conscience. Conscience appears to be the law that God has written on our hearts.

Another evidence of God is that of the spiritual and metaphysical world. The paranormal and supernatural happenings cannot currently be explained by science. There are the sightings of angels/spirits, the demon-possessed, the inexplicable healings, prophecies, speaking in tongues, visions and other miracles.

The sighting of angels or spirits can be explained as hallucinations if the sighting is only by one person. When the sighting is by more than one person, it cannot be explained as hallucinations. There has to be another explanation. Many people who have had near death experiences describe a world beyond death that is very much similar to that of heaven and hell as described in the Bible.

The demon-possessed have extraordinary strength and physical abilities, and special cognitive abilities such as reading of minds, giving accurate accounts of other people's histories and future happenings. As of current, their extraordinary abilities cannot be scientifically explained.

Other evidences of a spiritual world include inexplicable healings where cancer cells may inexplicably disappear, prophecies that have come true, tongues that are validated as obscure languages and visions that have uncanny resemblances to real happenings or objects.

Many people have shared their testimonies of how God has helped them. This book itself is a testimony of God's might, love, grace and mercy. Could these testimonies be coincidences or a product of imagination? There are just too many of these testimonies to explain them as coincidences. Moreover, many of the incidents are too uncanny to be explained as coincidences. Why then, does God help some but not others? I will attempt to explain this later.

Others have shared their testimonies of experiencing God. Experiencing God can be directly through your physical senses, indirectly by relation through happenings, or by your spiritual sense. Perhaps that was how the term "sixth sense" was born. "Sixth sense" refers to the spiritual sense through which you can communicate with God and other spiritual entities.

Is Jesus God?

If we are satisfied that there is God, then the question that will arise is "Who is God?" We have to look at the origins of the various religions. The great moral teachers include Jesus, Siddhartha, Buddha, Mohammad and Confucius. Of all these great moral teachers, only Jesus proclaimed himself as God; none others have claimed that they are God. The others either claim to be prophets to a God or are exalted by others as God. Most of the major religions have originated from these moral teachers. Only one has truly originated from the One who has proclaimed himself as God.

Could Jesus be a madman? It seems unlikely so as Jesus is someone with profound understanding of humanity. Moreover his actions have never indicated any perceptual or cognitive impairment characteristic of psychosis.

The birth, death and resurrection of Jesus had been prophesized by many who came before Him. Many events that occurred during His time validated the prophecies that came before Him. The prophecies also spoke of this person as God. We can thus infer that Jesus is God as there are countless evidences that He has fulfilled those prophecies.

Another evidence that Jesus is God is that His name has authority. In casting out demons from those who are possessed, His name has the ultimate authority. Demons are afraid of His name. His name also has the authority to perform other miracles such as healing of both a physical and psychological nature.

Is the Bible Authentic?

One of my main doubts has been whether the bible is authentic. Its authenticity in terms of its historical origin is without much doubt as recordings of historical events in other manuscripts are in line with those recorded in the Bible.

The different books in the Bible are written by different people. There are a lot of cross-references that validate the authenticity of one book written by one person by that of another book written by another person. It seems almost impossible that the Bible is fictitious and made up by one person or a group of persons as the depth and breath of knowledge (truth) is tremendous and it seems impossible for the Bible to be purely borne out of human contemplation. It seems more likely that the Bible is written based on revelation through God.

I have always wondered whether the Bible is the whole truth or part God's revelation and part fictitious imagination. From my own experience in writing this book, I have come to realize that in the same way as God has revealed the truth behind the *autistic spectrum disorder* to me, it is highly possible that God has revealed the whole truth to the different writers of the Bible. If God chose the Bible as the basis of our understanding of Him, He will certainly make sure that what is written in it is the whole truth.

Why does God allow Calamities and Illnesses?

In the beginning, there were no calamities and illnesses. It was only when we began to sin that we became separated from God. The fruit of separation and sin are calamities and illnesses. God did not create these abominations. God initially wanted people to be sinless and to be free from these abominations. That was His initial plan for us. It was because we turned away from Him and sinned that we are now loaded with these afflictions.

One example is how sin causes the *autistic spectrum disorder*. This disorder is caused by trauma and trauma is usually caused by sin. War, violence, rape and child abuse can all cause trauma and without doubt, they are all the children of sin. Horror and violent movies are the trademark of the dark one and can be categorically defined as sin. Other than for medical reasons where abortions contemplated are usually brought to fruition, contemplated abortions that are not eventually carried out are usually the result of immorality, rape, etc. These uncompleted abortions could lead to trauma and congenital *autism*.

Now that calamities and illnesses are already rampant, why does God not remove them? Perhaps that is because we have to bear the fruits of our sin. God also makes use of calamities and illnesses to bring us back to Him. It may only be when we suffer from some grievance that we eventually choose to depend on Him.

Sometimes, God also makes use of these grievances to test our resolve, perseverance, faith and dependence on Him. The world has now become a battlefield between good and evil. We need to be fully equipped in this battlefield to be able to stand firm.

Does God Listen?

For God to listen to our prayers and answer them, there are a few pre-requisites:

- It is within His plan.
- We are truly repentant of our sins.
- We love God and our neighbors.
- We follow His decrees.

- We abide by Him.

- We may have to be patient.

God's plan is the big picture. He is omniscient and can see the past, the present and the future. He can see all the primary and secondary effects and repercussions of answering our prayers. He knows our character and personalities well. He may already have a plan for us, whereas what we ask for may jeopardize His plans. We in turn have to abide in Him and His instructions.

If we are unrepentant of our sins, we become separated from God. When we become separated from God, He will not listen and answer our prayers. In the same way, if we do not love God and our neighbors, God will not listen to our prayers. Following God's decrees is just an extension of our love for God and our neighbors. It is our way of portraying our love. If we are truly repentant, we should follow God's decrees and in so doing, avoid sin, and showcase our love for Him and others.

God has His timing in answering prayers. Sometimes we may have to wait for some time before God answers our prayers. This period of time may be short or considerable. We have to be patient. After all, God took about four years to answer my prayer that I be healed from my affliction.

I hope that you too will be able to join me in enjoying the grace and love of God. "I pray this in Jesus' precious name, Amen."

10

Altered Personalities

Man with no backbone

One of the monikers that has often been used to describe me is that of having "no backbone". This has both physical and characterological connotations.

In the physical sense, it has been used to describe my tendency to "slouch" and my overall dishevelled disposition. I have of late attributed the origin of my slouch as being induced by the endocrinological malfunction. The slouch is probably a result of the serotogenic physical disturbances. That may also explain why slouching is usually associated with low self-confidence.

In secondary school, my hair was often messy and my shirt which was supposed to be tucked into my pants often came out. Similarly my shoelaces often came untied. Sometimes food stains appeared surreptitiously onto my clothing. It was not that I did not comb my hair in the morning, that my shirt came out more often than for others, or that my shoelaces were not tied hard enough. It was just that when my hair or clothes were messed up during the course of the day, I did not notice them and hence did not attempt to preen myself regularly.

My untidy gait also contributed to this ignominy. I usually took each step with my whole feet coming into contact with the ground all at the same time. This differs from normal people who would take their steps heel-first followed by their feet. My hands also hardly swung when I walked. Perhaps that also contributed to a sloppy gait as a person's swinging hands are meant to balance the moments of his body and hips.

Sloppy forgetfulness was also one of the characteristics as I frequently misplaced my wallet. I have lost count of the number of wallets that I lost and the penalties I have had to pay for replacement identity cards. It led to many inconveniences.

During Junior College, I took part in the 100 meters relay event for the athletics meet. I was running the last leg of the event. Taking the baton from my team-mate I began accelerating. I wanted to win. Because of my poor body sense, I did not realize that my upper torso was accelerating faster than my feet could follow. As I ran and ran, my body became more and more angled and eventually I toppled over. Prior to toppling over, I did not have any clue of my increasingly precarious position and was stunned when my feet actually gave way under me. It was a real embarrassment but fortunately I picked myself up in time and our team managed to finish with a bronze medal.

In the characterological sense, "no backbone" can denote indecision, lack of independence and irresponsibility. Indecision is apparent because of the lack of meaning attached to most activities and also the impaired understanding of social conventions. For example if someone asked me to make a decision, neither of the choices would make any difference to me unless I felt strongly about a particular option. I either felt strongly for something or did not feel anything at all. There are no "in-between" feelings. In most situations, as I had no emotions attached to the options, I had no preferences and that led to indecision.

Another reason for indecision is uncertainty about social conventions. My entire wardrobe was decided by my sister. I did not have an inkling into what clothes were socially acceptable, nor what were the prevailing trends. Neither did I have a clue about how to match one piece of apparel with another piece in terms of their colors, style and patterns. Often if left to my own devices, I would select tops and bottoms that are obviously mismatched to other people. Appreciating my own limitations, I left the buying of my clothes to my sister. She would then instruct me on which shirt can come with which pants and which shoes and so on and forth. I gladly followed her instructions.

Most of my major life decisions have also been about indecision. This includes selection of the schools that I enrolled in, the courses I took, as well as the employment that I subsequently undertook. Both the secondary school and junior college I enrolled in were decided by either my parents or sister. To me, these schools were just names and there was no difference where I went. There was no meaning attached to any of these names. It did not even come across my mind that I should find out more about these schools and what they had to offer. Schools were just schools and I could not fathom the differences in them. Likewise when I applied for entrance into the University, I first applied for a place in the Law faculty. I did not choose the faculty but it was my sister who urged me on that choice. Owing to my poor interview skills, my application was not accepted. I then applied for Engineering which was the safest option and which our Government strongly advocated then due to the high demand for Engineers.

In the same way, my subsequent employment was left to fate. I sieved through the recruitment ads and applied for any job that was suitable for my course of study. I had not much clue as to what those jobs really represented in relation to their suitability for me or whether I was interested in them. I had this fear that I was unable to secure employment due to my impairment and disabilities. "Any job will do", I thought to myself.

Lack of independence is apparent due to the constricted nature of my consciousness. I was not independent because I did not know how to respond to unique situations and could only function within my small sphere of understanding. As the Chinese saying goes, I was like the "frog in the well". Just like the frog that could not see what was happening outside the well, I had a narrow perception and understanding of the external realities and was apathetic to anything beyond my boundaries. There was an invisible barrier of separation. It was as if I could only assimilate anything that had a pattern into my memory. There was difficulty in assimilating everything else that did not fit into these patterns. Depending on the nature and my degree of involvement, things that happened outside of these boundaries either induced apathy or anxiety.

Irresponsibility is a natural extension of dependence. In many situations, in order to be responsible, I had to function outside of those boundaries. If I was asked to do something outside of these boundaries and there was no attached anxiety, I would just obey and carry it out. However if it was the responsible thing to do but nobody prompted me to do it, I would not carry it out as the thought does not even enter into my consciousness. I was with no initiative and portrayed a lackadaisical attitude. Sometimes when anxiety was attached to a particular situation outside of these boundaries, even if somebody asked me to do something and it was the responsible thing to do, I would conveniently gloss over or forget about my responsibilities. The anxiety was too much to bear and even though I knew that I ought to be responsible, the anxiety triumphed over responsibility.

During one situation in secondary one, my teacher had wrongly corrected my examination paper and the error was costly as it meant a substantial difference in grades. I did not have the courage to question her about the error and left it as it was until all our marks were finalized and our "end-of-year" report card was issued. After the report card was issued, I did not know how to explain my poor results to my parents so I showed them the mistake that the teacher had made. In the end, my parents approached the teacher and she had to retrospectively amend my report card and re-issue it again. I was reprimanded for my irresponsible behaviour.

Peter Pan

When I was young I was named "Peter Chiang". It was only just prior to Junior College that I changed my name to "Irving Chiang". This was the outcome of my mother's consultation with an expert in numerology who calculated that it was necessary for me to change my name to alter my luck and fortune. The Chinese believed that people are made up of five elements: water, fire, earth, wood and gold. These elements depend on your birth date and time, your name and other major aspects of your life and relationships. In my case, I lacked "earth". Hence my name was changed to contain more "earth" in it. I do not believe in such superstitions but I went along as I did not have any opinion on the change of name and was apathetic to any impact on my identity and associations.

Over the years, I have had friends who described me as being childlike and never growing up. These friends were acquaintances both before and after the change in my name and hence my former name did not have any influence on the generalization of the description. "Peter Pan" was the boy who never grew up. I wondered then whether my former name had any connection to my personality.

During Junior College, prior to onset of the depression, one friend described me as such:

> "Irving. The kid of the lot. Childish, hyperactive. What else can I say? You are the most energetic and spirited......One day you will have to grow up and abandon this little kid. But one thing you must realize. Never let the kid die. He may not be what you will be, but keep him inside, for he shall be what that guides you through times of darkness. Treasure what you have, for what you have is rare amongst people. And cherish that innocence that I sought that you have. You have touched the little boy in me and awoken him and I think you have touched many more than me......"

I later found out that this friend of mine is homosexual. I wonder whether the little boy I touched in him could have awoken his homosexuality. Little though did my friend realize that what he was describing was a "sheep in wolf's clothing"; while the innocence seemed pure and attractive then, once I grew up and abandoned the little kid, this same innocence became the fruit of intense despair.

Upon the onset of acute trauma and the endocrinological malfunction, it was as if my personality and consciousness failed to grow anymore. In many ways, I was still trapped in the child-like personality of a ten-year old. It is the difficulty in integrating new experiences into explicit and narrative memory that results in procrastination of mental maturity. I could only integrate experiences into implicit memory (process or pattern oriented). This meant that things had to follow a pattern or I had to deliberately fit it into a pattern before I could assimilate it into my consciousness. For example, in the selection of clothes to wear, if someone tells me that blue always doesn't go with brown, I would then register the pattern into my memory and I can then remember not to wear brown tops with blue pants, etc. This way of learning takes longer. There is also less of "self" as you become more and more a "copy" of others.

A person's memory is constructed by his experiences. His memory plays a large part in determining his identity. A person's memory can be divided into explicit and implicit memory. Implicit memory is the memory used to remember facts, patterns and fixed processes and which a person later draws from to respond to fixed situations; a person's explicit memory is where the person deposits his experiences into his entire life story and which he later on draws from to respond to unique situations. You can think of implicit memory as parallel circuits (each pattern makes up a parallel circuit). Every time there is a new experience that justifies a previously observed pattern, it will add to the circuit in parallel. On the other hand, explicit memory is like a circuit in series (it keeps on adding up). Every time there is a new experience, it appends itself in series to memory.

In my case, there was impairment in explicit memory. I had difficulty appending new experiences into explicit memory. I could either assimilate experiences as a pattern or remember it as an event that happened but that is discrete from my other memories. There was a lack of integration of new experiences into explicit memory and that also resulted in the stunted growth of my personality.

There is some debate whether this impairment may affect creativity. Creativity can be inherent in a person's psyche or learned from experiences. In most areas of my life, I have often lacked creativity. Most of the time, I am not able to respond creatively to unique situations. However when I am able to perceive a pattern and apply it to the situation, sometimes this pattern can be considered creative. I also believe that creativity can also be inherent. An autistic individual being emotionally, sensually and socially detached from his surroundings would have to draw from his inner creativity. While a normal person's self and creativity may be tainted and influenced by the world around him. It is less so for an autistic individual as his forced separation may induce him to draw from inherent resources which are being less defined by the world and may appear abstract and sometimes inconceivable. This could be perceived by others as creativity. For example, it can be said that I am creative and innovative on the basis of my discovery of the cause and cure of the *autistic spectrum disorder.*

Two-faced Buddha

In secondary school, a few friends described me as "the person who is never angry". I realize it to be partially true because in school I was never angry with anyone. I never had any temper tantrums. Even if people offended me, I was either oblivious to the offence or remained unmoved by the affront. I wondered then why I was so passive and did not react in anger to situations.

There was however some differences when I was at home. Even though I never flew into terrible rages, I was often easily irritable. This irritableness was usually associated with disruptions in routine. For example, if I had planned to play video games or read a book at home after school and my mother who drove me from school detoured elsewhere for a while to run some errands, I would feel really irritated. If midway through reading my book and my mom asks me to help with household chores I would also feel irritation.

I wondered then why there were differences in school and at home. Was I being a hypocrite? Was I an actor in school and a monster at home? I now realize that it was in the relaxed environment of home that I usually followed my own routines and disruptions in these routines would trigger irritability. On the other hand, school was different. What I carried out in school was under the instructions of the school and my teachers. I had no control and just submissively followed orders with no tinge of irritation.

I sometimes felt that I was not being filial because I was always so reluctant to help my mother out in the chores or in running other errands. I could not however dispense with the irritability as it was then a natural reaction.

Other than routines that had to be adhered, I also had the tendency to follow rules inflexibly. For example, I was always strictly punctual for school and other appointments. Even if something may have happened that delayed the journey to school and I had a good excuse for being late; where my mother may have fallen sick or there was a massive traffic jam, I would still get irritated with the perpetrator for making me break the rules. My mother who was ill should be subject to my sympathies but instead became the cornerstone of my subtle wrath.

Himbo

One of my teachers (English Language) gave me a nickname, "Himbo", which is the male version of the "Bimbo". In the context of the Chinese, I had the looks of a "pretty boy" when I was younger. Whenever my teacher called me to answer a question in class, I would stand up and be totally confused as to what was the answer. I would make a complete fool of myself. The answer could be something that she had just mentioned but because I hardly paid attention in class, I did not know the answer. Not that I did not try to pay attention, it was just that her incessant verbal mutterings did not seem to register in my mind. In every class, as I could not really absorb what was being taught, I was either dreaming about something else, or counting down the minutes to recess break or end of school hours, when I could return back to my usual routines.

Other than not listening in class, I also did not do much of my homework. Most of my homework was copied either before or after class from my class-mates. I had to frequently try to insert some originality into the homework. My hyperactive self prevented me from dutifully completing my own home-work. Even when I had nothing else better to do, I would still refuse to touch my books. Hence, other than studying for tests or examinations, I hardly ever touched my schoolbooks.

This teacher was also in charge of the extra-curricular activity (ECA) of tennis which I took part in. I took part in tennis also because my mother suggested it. She felt that learning tennis was beneficial in that I could exercise and remain healthy, and that it could also prove useful in future in business and social sit-uations. Even though I joined tennis for four years, at the end of the four years, my tennis was no better than those who just joined the ECA. That was also the partial reason why my teacher looked upon me with derision.

My failure in tennis had to do with my impairment of senses and anxiety. I could not see the ball clearly when it came near me and would just hit out at it at its general location. When I tried to focus on the ball, I could not focus on my body and hand movements, and I could not focus on where I wanted to hit the ball. Needless to say, I was also little aware of my opponent and where he was. In tennis, it is necessary to be aware of the ball, the entire court, your opponent and your bodily movements all at the same time and that proved difficult for me. Anxiety made it worse. While I could still hit the ball across the net in friendly play, anxiety that came with competitive tennis proved even more disastrous as I performed far worse even by my usually poor standards.

I was a little offended by my teacher's remarks that I was a "Himbo" and decided to proof her wrong. Even though I still did not do my homework, I started to read intensively to brush up my English. From then on, reading science fiction novels also became one of the natural routines. I also started putting in more efforts into studying for my examinations and the result was an exemplary academic performance in my GCE "O" levels, the intermediate examinations for entrance into Junior College.

Initially even though I read a lot, I had difficulty remembering and applying words and my vocabulary remained poor. Perhaps this had some relation to the learning and memory disabilities symptomatic of *autism*. I decided to memorize bombastic words and their applications, and force them into my compositions. These words did not revolve around the story line but rather the story line revolved around my words. I wrote the story to fit in with the words used, rather than that the words were used to fit in with the story. Overtime, this proved effective as these words were forcefully ingrained into my subconscious.

"Yes" man

Whenever people asked me about something, for example, do you want to eat this or do you want to do this? I mostly answered yes. Unless it was an unreasonable request, or I had a particular distaste for it or that it was morally wrong, I did not usually have any strong feelings about any of the choices nor did I really conceive further into the implications of agreeing with their proposition. As I did not have strong feelings about these choices and being oblivious to social cues and body language, I was uncertain whether in that social context I would be offensive if I rejected their goodwill. Thus, I was mostly agreeable. As a result, I became known as the "Yes" man. Sometimes though, after having agreed to the proposition and when I was actually acting in accordance to my promises, I would realize that what I agreed to was not what I really wanted and I would begin to regret having made that promise.

Usually I would have one good friend at any one phase of my life. I could only cope with one good friend at any one time. It was less of a friend-to-friend relationship but more of a leader-to-follower relationship. I was the follower. I could only have one good friend at any one time because often I could only be agreeable to one person. For example, one friend might ask me to watch a movie while another might ask me to go bowling. I could not possibly split myself into two. Hence, I could not agree to both sides but I did not know who to reject as I was afraid I would offend either one of the two parties. I also did not have any preference for any of the two activities. I did not know how to handle such situations and naturally I became a "one good friend" person.

Outside of my own restricted interests and routines, I did not know what else to do and how to fit in with my peers and the trend. I began to rely on my good friends as bridges to the real world.

The friendships did not last for long as I was more of a zombie than a real person. After some time, my good friend would become bored of me because I did not produce fresh ideas, I did not reciprocate emotionally, my mentality did not progressively mature in line with our increasing age and I did not assimilate naturally with other peers. It was because of this and my own helplessness that I latched on to "one good friend" after another. I became almost dependent on others to define my own identity that was very much obscure.

There was once when a good friend in secondary school started to ignore me. I was full of angst. Initially, prior to befriending him, I was happy with my life and satisfied with following my own routines and keeping to my restricted interests. It was through him that I realized how different reality should be like and what I was really missing in life. He was the one who brought me to the movies, shopping, restaurants, cafes, arcades, parties and holidays and he opened my eyes to the real world. The revelation had brought me beyond the small sphere in which my psyche previously existed and into a larger world where I could envisage the actual realities but because of my disabilities, I could not actively partake in.

"Sotong"

Sotong is squid in Malay. In our culture, it is a pseudonym for being very "blur". Some friends used to call me "Sotong" because I had little sense of direction and frequently did not know how to handle new situations. If someone directed me to take public bus to a place I had not been to by bus before, I would likely find myself lost. Even if I had been to that place by bus before but I was then with another person, I would also likely find myself lost. If I had previously found my own way to the new place by bus, I could still get lost on a subsequent visit. Most of the time, I either took the public bus with a friend who knows the way, or my mother would drive me there. If I was alone, I would only take the public bus on familiar routes.

One thing about taking public buses alone was that there was an anxiety attached to it. Our public bus system requires us to press a bell when we are nearing our destination and only then would the bus driver stop the bus for passengers to alight. If I took the bus alone, I always had difficulty judging when to press the bell. I had this difficulty with judging distances and was always uncertain whether the bus was nearing the next bus stop and when was an appropriate time to press the bell. When the time came for me to press the bell, tension and anxiety would well up inside me. Frequently I procrastinated for too long and the bus would zoom pass the bus stop that I wanted to alight at. Consequently, I often had to walk one or two bus stops back to where I actually wanted to alight. Eventually on those regular bus routes I took, I had fixed markers as to when I would press the bell. If I wanted to stop at this particular bus stop, I would press the bell once the bus went pass a particular landmark that was situated at an appropriate distance from the designated bus stop.

The difficulty in judging distances was not only restricted to getting off the bus. There was also a similar predicament when I was at the bus stop and waving for the public bus to stop. I was not able to judge when was an appropriate time to stick out my hands to wave for the bus to stop. Sometimes, I would stick out my hands too late and by which time the bus driver had insufficient time to react. The bus driver would either ignore me or he would jam his brakes to stop the bus some distance ahead of the bus stop. Many bus drivers have glared at me angrily whilst I clambered onto their buses.

Moving around in school wasn't much of a problem as after a while, I became familiar with the entire compound. During lessons all I had to do was to follow instructions when there were instructions. During recess breaks, I would just go to the cafeteria in the same way as I did everyday. It had become a routine. After school, I would either go home or just follow my good friend to wherever he was going. If the situation suddenly changed and taking a fictitious scenario where I would have to go alone to the airport and board the plane to another country, I am sure I would be totally lost. Firstly I would have trouble getting to the airport. Without my mother to drive me, I had no clue how to call a cab. Even if I managed to reach the airport, I would probably not know that I had to check in my luggage and so on and so forth. Clearly, I was not able to function adequately in a new or unique environment.

Ice Man

After I became depressed in Junior College, I was no longer the enigmatic kid that my friends had previously described me as. I was forced to grow up and became very introspective. I knew that I had a problem. I became depressed and from then on it was all about me rationalizing my own problems. From the outside, people would perceive me as always being apprehensive and deep in thought. I had become even less responsive to external stimulus. Before I became depressed, I already had my disabilities, but as these disabilities did not bother my way of life, they did not pose any obstacles to my lifestyle. I was also non-the-wiser to my impairment. It was at this moment that I gradually and intuitively knew that I was different from others and I knew that I would never fit into society. I became passive and reserved. Everything that happened around me seemed to bounce off me. I retreated into my own shell.

There was this game that I played with my orientation group in the University. The game involved each of us being distributed a note. We than had to write our individual names on our own note. The note was then passed around in a circle and all the people in the circle had to add one word to describe the person that the note represented. The following are the collated results on my note:

- Reliable (1)
- Good Looking (1)
- Smart (1)
- Observant (2)
- Trustworthy (1)
- Sincere (1)
- Good in what he does (1)

- No confidence (1)

- Quiet and reserved (8)

- Mysterious (1)

It was obvious then that "Ice Man" is an appropriate pseudonym as I was always quiet and reserved and I was not very responsive to what was happening around me. Ironically, "observant" appeared twice because I was hypersensitive and particularly observant to certain aspects of my surroundings and what was happening. I was however oblivious to most of the other aspects of what was happening.

When it came to conversations with other people, most of the time I would not talk and just listen. Moments of silence were torturous to me and I would try to fill up these moments with questions or prompts for the other party to continue on their monologue. This was how conversations with others were established during this period.

Another problem came with greeting acquaintances. Greeting acquaintances that are met in the streets and colleagues in the office usually comes naturally to most people. It is however of great difficulty for me. When I meet people that I know on the streets, I would try to avoid them. What I should say to them or even in what manner of body language I should express my greeting does not come naturally to me. Sometimes when it becomes unavoidable, I have to conceive a strategy to extend my greeting. I would choose between smiling, nodding my head or waving my hands or just saying "Hi". Whether by way of verbal expression or through body language, my greetings usually end up being constricted; my greetings can either end up being too subtle or over exaggerated.

In the office, I often meet my colleagues more than once a day. After greeting the colleague in the morning, I might see him again at other times of the day. I am frequently unsure how I should react in such situations and whether I should greet the person again. I try to look away and pretend not to see the person.

Sometimes people that I see once and find in them a sense of familiarity and affinity, I would attempt to greet them on the streets when I see them again, only to realize that they do not recognize me. On the other hand, other people that I meet every day in the lift and that recognize me, I do not greet them because of the lack of affinity. After a few experiences of being snubbed by the "familiar" people, I have become more uncertain as to whether or not I should greet the person if I do recognize them. There is difficulty in judging those people that are in a sense "greetable".

Busybody

I was quiet and reserved and hardly responded to most of my external stimuli. Despite that, I was sometimes considered a busybody, especially by the girls who liked to gossip. With the hypersensitivity mixed with the impairment of senses, even as I was some distance away from the girls who were gossiping, I could pick up one or two words that were being said and this incited my curiosity. I would then go up to them and ask them what it was all about. However I would only ask questions and did not provide any material for their conversations. I was very persistent in satisfying my curiosity and kept on asking until I was satisfied with the answers. I could hardly be considered conversational as my conversations were only inquisitory in nature. This occurred frequently and I became known as the "busybody".

In the rustle and bustle of crowded places such as pubs, I could not partake in any conversation. In the cacophony of the ambient background noise, I could hardly make out what other people were saying and frequently I just nodded my head to acknowledge that the other person was saying something even though I had little clue of what he was conveying. Sometimes when I perceived that the other person was trying to crack a joke, I would pretend to laugh even though I did not know what was so comical.

Recluse

My social impairment was exhibited in three forms, each associated with different categories of associations. These associations can be categorized into three types, as follows:

- Friends who shared my restricted interests;
- Friends whose interests I had adopted in the "leader-follower" relationship; and
- All other associations.

Prior to the onset of realization and depression, I could effectively relate and communicate with the first two categories of people. With friends who shared my interests, there was a commonality upon which we had basis to communicate. With friends whose interests I had assimilated in the "leader-follower" relationship, I had to some extent adopted their persona and there was also some commonality upon which we could relate to each other. With all other associations who did not share my restricted interests and that I did not know well enough to assimilate their interests, there was no communality upon which we could relate to each other and effectively communicate. My lack of emotional empathy had a disabling effect on this aspect of social relations. I could not relate to the emotional aspects of their experiences which is vital in social interaction.

Hypersensitivity and impairment of my senses also had some disabling effect on communication. In a noisy environment or an environment where there are other distracting stimuli, there was difficulty in concentrating on the conversation. Moreover verbal communication requires simultaneous responses: listening to the conversation; looking at the other party; interpreting his body language; thinking about what to say; and actually putting the words into my mouth. This necessity for simultaneous responses proved difficult with the lack of proper sensory and thought integration.

When it came to people in the third category, I would do my utmost best to avoid them in social situations (such as parties, functions, etc) as I had nothing better to say to them and there was difficulty in maintaining eye contact. Sometimes, my parents' associates would visit us at our home and I would frequently hole myself up in the toilet in a bid to avoid them. The inability to socially interact with them often left me in the toilet feeling rather anxious and disorientated.

As my friends matured, their identities grew and their interests changed. I could not keep up with these changes as my personality had become immobilized immediately after the onset of the endocrinological malfunction. More and more of my friends were moving from the first two categories to the third category of associations. Why was my personality unable to grow as others could? This was when I realized that I was "different" and as this realization sank in, I grew depressed.

Upon this realization that I was different, my relations with others grew more and more contrived. There was little hope and meaning to life and my own interests had become less and less important. I just wanted to be normal and to be like others. I was being cornered into a cul-de-sac. While instinctively I had to have some restricted interests to give meaning to my life and to reduce anxieties, yet these same interests held no meaning in my newfound perception of actual reality.

I became dumfounded and an empty vessel. I did not know who was the real me. My relationships faltered. I had become an actor even in front of close family relations. I felt contrived in the presence of family members. I did not know myself, did not know how I should react and did not know what to say. Everything had become an act and was carried out so that I appeared responsive. I had become anxious even in the presence of my own family members as I did not know how to respond and yet had to conjure up a response to appear normal.

My social awkwardness, avoidance and anxieties are best portrayed by the choice of hair salons that I visited. When my hair grew long and I had to trim it, I would never go to the same hair salon more than a few times. I did not want to become too familiar with the hairstylist as I was awkward with familiarity. I felt uncomfortable when the hairstylist asked me personal questions as I did not know how to respond. To prevent things from getting too personal, after not more than two sessions with the same stylist, I would hunt for a new location to cut my hair.

Timid Mouse

With the inability to function adequately in a unique environment, often I had to have someone to accompany me in carrying out the necessary functions in life. There was an anxiety associated with having to independently carry out a function that was unique and that I had difficulty coping with. One of these necessary functions was shopping for clothes and other unique items such as gifts. There are just too many shopping places in the country and too large variety of clothes or possible gifts for selection. The line of clothes changes frequently and each new line provide a unique situation. The vast possibilities of gifts and unique items also left me absolutely flabbergasted. The large variety of shopping places also made each individual shopping place largely unique and unfamiliar to my consciousness.

Hence when it came to shopping for these items, I could not shop alone and there was an anxiety related to it. There was an inability to cope with and respond to the unique environment due both to the situational impairment of senses and the failure of assimilating previous experiences in application to the current situation. There was also an inability to judge the appropriateness of the purchases. All these contributed to the disability and an associated anxiety. There was then a dependence on others to make up for this shortfall.

When I first bought flowers for my girlfriend, I did not know where to buy the flowers and what flowers to buy. Other considerations were cost and I did not want to get cheated. In the end, I decided on the safe choice of buying roses. It was obvious that roses symbolized romance and I did not know of any other appropriate flowers. I was also too proud to ask others. I did not have an inkling of where I could purchase flowers although on many previous occasions, I had walked pass florists but I was just not aware of them. I did not ask others to accompany me because of my pride and because I felt that this was something I had to do by myself as I very much wanted to be independent. Eventually after much anxiety, I managed to locate a florist and bought the flowers. I must qualify though that the flowers were bought more because I perceived that my girlfriend demanded them rather than that I bought them based on my own initiative.

One difficulty that came with buying gifts was that I lacked empathy and could not judge whether the gift was appropriate for use by the receiver. Another difficulty was that because of the impairment of the senses, I could not when buying the gift, judge whether the item was aesthetically pleasant. The sensual difficulty also extended to buying my own clothes. I could not judge whether the clothes I bought for myself were aesthetically pleasant and sometimes I could not judge whether these clothes fit well. I have on many occasions bought clothes that I later realize do not fit well or shoes that are too big. Most of the time I bought oversized items as when I was trying on these items, I judge the adequacy of their sizes more in terms of their touch and feel rather than sight. I usually bought oversized clothes and shoes because of my hypersensitivity to touch and my lack of tolerance for clothes and shoes that are too tight.

When it came to straightforward items such as toothbrushes, shavers, etc, I had no difficulty as I could always buy these items from the same store and in the same manner.

There was also an associated anxiety when asking people simple questions of information. In the usual necessities of life, questions often had to be asked to find out information. This could be at service counters or by telephone through the call centres. For example, I may need to find out the terms and conditions of my hand phone service plan. Even these trivial questions were met with anxiety. If the information was not essential, I would just make do without the information and find ways around it. If the information was essential, I would prepare myself a script of what I wanted to say in advance, remember it and recite it when the time came. When I did not prepare my speech in advance, my sentences usually appear disjointed and I often had to repeat myself a few times before the other party could understand me.

Addict

It is not surprising that with the shortfall in senses and emotions, I became addicted to activities that accentuated the "elation" that could replace this shortfall. Prior to the depression, I initially became addicted to playing video games. At the same time, masturbation had almost become an addiction. Other activities were later added to this list and what they all had in common was to give me the same false sense of pleasure.

During the depression, most of these previous activities that I had indulged in had no meaning to me anymore. I still continued to indulge in a few of those activities that gave me a raw sense of thrill and pleasure. In the army, I also began to indulge in gambling. Gambling gave me a sense of raw thrill that could momentarily fill up the emptiness inside me. Even then, it did not proof an effective replacement as it was transient and not exactly the same as what it sought to replace.

This same shortfall can also explain some of the addictions of autistic individuals. Autistic individuals are more susceptible to alcoholism and drug abuse. They may also be addicted to sex and masturbation. There are also many others who willingly succumb to being bullied and those who self-mutilate. Their purpose and goal are all the same and that is to stimulate a sense of feeling in them, to make sense of life and to reduce their anxieties.

Bone Cracker

Even though I did not exhibit the repetitive actions typical of autistic individuals such as hand clapping, head banging, etc, I had my own expressions of repetitive and ritualistic behaviours. My expressions of these behaviours could in other contexts appear normal.

One of these repetitive actions was that of cracking of my bones. Every joint in my body that could be cracked, I have attempted to crack. I would patiently go through the entire array of joints (fingers, toes, ankles, knee caps, wrists, and elbows) and after cracking each joint once, these joints would become silent and I would wait for the next opportunity when the joint once again re-establishes its ability to produce the cracking sound. This became a ritualistic action as I would crack every single joint that can be cracked and then repeat this once again when the cracking sound returns to the joint.

There are a few other joints that I have attempted to crack but am usually unsuccessful. Rarely though I do manage to crack them and this gives me an intense sense of satisfaction. This includes the shoulders, spine and the neck. After I got attached to my girlfriend, I sometimes held hands with her. On many such occasions I also attempted to crack the joints of her fingers. Clearly, this repetitive action of cracking joints was not restricted to only my own joints.

Other than joint cracking, I did not portray any other obvious ritualistic actions. However I did have the tendency to carry out some actions that can be related to anxiety and hyperactivity. One of this was the frequent shaking of my legs while I was sitting. Another was my penchant for rubbing my feet together while I was lying on my bed just before I slept. Still another was my fondness of standing on one leg while I brushed my teeth. I just could not stand still on two legs! Eventually I did stop standing on one leg to brush my teeth but I had to do something else while brushing my teeth as it was just too boring. I either had to take a shower while brushing my teeth or walked around the house while doing so. I just could not stay still!

There was a period though when I particularly liked to squeeze out the pimples on my hands and legs. I am not sure whether this too can be considered as a ritualistic behaviour.

Another exhibition of ritualistic behaviour was perhaps my fondness for counting. I would count the number of cars that drove past before my parents came home. I would count the number of steps that I took to reach a certain destination. From the balcony of my apartment, I could see the swimming pool and I would frequently count the number of people in the swimming pool. Sometimes when I was in commercial complexes such as hotels or offices, I would count the number of repeated patterns on the floor or wall tiles.

My penchant for the cracking of joints was an expression of my anxiety and hyperactivity. In contrast, counting was just a way of making sense of the world in which I felt disconnected.

Chameleon

At the depths of my despair when my depression was at its worse, I did not know how to react in situations and respond to external stimuli and people. I did not have any innate personality and without any personality, it was not possible for me to interact with others. I had to subsume other people's personality to appear to function normally in front of family and friends. This was done by mimicking other peoples' personalities and characteristics as an exterior that could hide the emptiness beneath it.

I was particularly envious of one of my friends who was very popular amongst our peers. His popularity had to do with his emotional empathy and the care and concern he showed others, but at that time I perceived his popularity to be his witty nature and the jokes that he often cracked. With this perception and in an effort to emulate him, I began to crack jokes at every social situation. My jokes were however brainless and inappropriate. Often they were not befitting of the situation and created an awkward atmosphere.

In the same way, I tried to emulate many others during this period. I would take on part of one person's personality that I felt could attract friends and another person's personality that I felt was indicative of how I should act at my age and of my perceived social status. I was in effect like a "chameleon" that tried to blend in and camouflage into the background. My personality had become mostly the combination of bits and pieces of other peoples' personalities.

If others went Europe for a holiday after graduating, I felt I too had to go to Europe for a holiday after graduating. If others were invited to parties, I very much wanted to be invited to parties. If others took part in University orientation camps, I also wanted to take part in the camps. I just wanted to assimilate or appear to do so with my peers.

I also plagiarized other people's opinion by taking snippets of what others told me and used their interesting opinions as my own opinions in conversations with other people. There was little originality in my expressions of personal opinions.

Hypochondriac

There was a period shortly after the traumatic experience that I frequently wondered whether I could have contracted a terminal illness. Every day, I would be worried that I had contracted a terminal illness such as cancer or AIDS, etc. This worrisome behaviour was extremely exaggerated. For example, because of hormonal changes, during that time I detected some lumps under my armpits. I was very worried that I had contracted cancer and hastened to tell my parents about my discovery. I related this new discovery to the other physical symptoms that I had experienced not long after the traumatic incident, and was convinced that there was really something amiss with my health.

My parents were sceptical that it was cancer but nonetheless brought me to consult a doctor. The doctor assured me that these lumps were normal and all part of me growing up. I was not convinced by his explanation and continued to agonize over my dire predicament and remained deeply disturbed.

Genius

Some people have perceived me to be intelligent while others have found me foolish and immature. There were two sides of the coin. On one side, I was the genius who could solve complex mathematical problems in a simplistic manner. On the other side, I was the fool that was not streetwise and had little emotional intelligence.

My mathematics teacher in Junior College told the whole class that he thought that I was a genius. The methodologies with which I had used to solve mathematical problems were unique and innovative, sometimes different from what was being taught. It is not uncommon that autistic individuals perform better at tasks that are self-taught rather than those that they learn from others. In the same way, the methodologies which I employed for solving these problems were always using variations of the first principles and my own logic, and not the way that it was taught in class.

The autistic individual has a disability in assimilating what is being taught by others into his memory. To compensate for this, there is a reliance on his personal reserves to self-learn. Consequently autistic individuals may have strange solutions for solving problems that may seem peculiar to the normal person. There are those with *asperger's syndrome* that have been awarded with the Nobel Prize. Their atypical thinking and the intensity of their interests could have contributed to their innovative discoveries.

I remember someone once asked me how I thought. My reply to him was that I just thought. The ideas seem to come to me from nowhere and suddenly appear at the tip of my consciousness. The bottom layers of my consciousness where the ideas were formulated I did not seem to have access to. By the time I was aware of the ideas, they were already processed and ready to be applied. It was as if in my autistic state, I had a larger subconscious which did most of the work and at the same time a narrowing of my conscious mind. That was the only part of my mind I was aware of and which served as the platform for application of my ideas.

Zombie

Having no emotions is the signature characteristic of a zombie. I was of little emotion. Not long after the traumatic incident, my father was posted to Hong Kong for his work. We remained in Singapore as our studies were not to be disrupted. Some time later, my father returned to Singapore to visit us. I remember my perception of him as a complete stranger. I felt awkward and was not sure how I should react to his newfound presence. He had been gone for less than a year but during that time I had almost totally forgotten about his existence.

I remember attending my grandfather's funeral in secondary school. During that time, I did not feel sad at all and wondered to myself whether I was being evil for not feeling any emotions. From my vantage point, I could see the tears and misery of my other relatives but yet I did not feel a wee bit of emotion. It was somewhat similar when my father passed away in year 2001 when I just graduated. This time round I felt some sadness but the depth of emotion was not commensurate with the significant distress of the situation.

I also had an affected way in which I responded to polite questions of good-will. People would ask me how was I, and I would just respond by saying "fine". This was despite the fact that I could not relate my life to the word "fine" and what it really meant. I was previously taught to reply in such a way and from thenceforth have always employed "fine" as a useful answer for such questions. I have never taken the initiative to elaborate further.

I have always felt awkward when people showed me affection and concern. I would feel really uncomfortable and try to wriggle my way out of the situation. I also felt embarrassed when people praised me or whenever I was at the centre of their attention.

Disliking being at the centre of attention, I seldom celebrated my birthday. I did not like being the person that everyone was talking about and paying attention to. It made me feel like squirming and wishing that I was safely tucked away in a faraway place. Birthdays also did not hold much of any meaning to me. In the earlier years of my problem, the only things that held meaning to me were the restricted repertoire of activities that I revelled in. Subsequently when I realized my own difficulties and grew introspective, I did hope to have people to celebrate my birthday with as the lack thereof signified my inability to have any friends.

After the realization set in that I was dysfunctional, I kept my distance from people who tried to befriend or get close to me. I knew my own limitations and felt that I should not let anyone get close to me. Nobody would want a friend who had no identity and personality. I knew that in trying to befriend me they were judging me only based on first impressions. Second and third impressions would reveal the vast emptiness that I actually was.

My lack of emotions can also be observed by how I act in front of the camera. The cameraman would prompt me to smile but I just cannot smile. No matter how hard I tried, my smile never seems natural. My photographs always turn up with me either looking very solemn or with an unnatural curl to my lips that does not appear to look much like a smile.

11

Dialectic of Trauma

Effects of Trauma

Trauma affects people in different ways and varying degrees. What is considered a normal reaction to trauma and what is considered as a disorder? The normal reaction to trauma could be a period following the trauma that comprises of the following symptoms:

- Anxiety
- Fear
- Denial
- Avoidance
- Anger
- Withdrawal
- Insomnia
- Nightmares
- Hypervigilance and startle
- Painful thoughts and memories

What then is the difference between the normal response to trauma, post traumatic illnesses and *post traumatic stress disorder*? Normal response to trauma can be recognized as a response that is temporary and does not result in significant dysfunction. *Post traumatic stress disorder* is defined by the full range of prolonged autonomic responses that includes anxiety, fear, intrusive memories, withdrawal, hypervigilance and startle, and that these responses result in significant dysfunction. Post traumatic illnesses can be considered as mental disorders resulting from the trauma other than *post traumatic stress disorder*. Some of these mental illnesses are also often diagnosed in people who have not apparently suffered from trauma and hence are perceived not to be necessarily caused by trauma. These illnesses include anxiety disorders, personality disorders, mood disorders and substance abuse disorders. Post traumatic illnesses can also be found com-morbid with *post traumatic stress disorder*. They are not mutually exclusive.

Aetiology of PTSD

The diagnosis of PTSD currently requires the presence of major or catastrophic stressors as a criterion. There is however insufficient evidence to show that PTSD is uniquely associated with extraordinary stressors.[1] Some studies have shown that PTSD does not only occur when the stressor is extraordinary severe.[2] There are patients who exhibit all of the symptoms of PTSD but have not experienced any major or catastrophic event. Rather, the onset of these symptoms was triggered by less severe stressors. These stressors could include idiopathic illnesses, apparently uncomplicated medical procedures, and normal loss events. Some studies have shown that not all of the variance of PTSD was explained by the nature and extent of the stressor. A 40% variance of PTSD was explained by the presence of combat exposure in one study,[3] and a 28% variance was explained in another study.[4] It is obvious that the "stressor" only plays a partial role in the explanation of PTSD. The person's personality, experiences, genetic pre-disposition and most importantly his perception of the traumatic event also likely explain the development of PTSD. Both personality and pre-existing factors can affect the person's perception of the traumatic event and influence the risk of developing PTSD. It is reasonable to conceive that some people can perceive "stressors" seemingly minor in pathological terms to have huge impact on their lives, and this perception can lead to PTSD.

Some studies have shown that previous or pre-existing mental illnesses can increase the likelihood of PTSD on subsequent exposure to traumatic events.[5] Other studies refute this claim and indicate that there is insufficient evidence that previous or pre-existing mental illnesses increase the rate of PTSD.[6] Even if studies have shown relation between previous mental illnesses and PTSD, this could be because the same genetic, personality and pre-existing factors could pre-dispose the person to both the occurrence of PTSD and the occurrence of the earlier acquired mental illnesses. It may not be the presence of these previous or pre-existing mental illnesses per-se that pre-disposes the person to developing PTSD or other post traumatic illnesses.

In the studies of personality factors as a predictor of PTSD, it was found that introverted and neurotic people are most likely victims of PTSD.[7] It could be that this personality sub-type may incline the person to magnify the meaning attached to the traumatic event, or that he may have less social support that can help to prevent or alleviate PTSD. Neurotic people are less carefree and more worrisome, and are socially less active. On the other hand, the correlation of this personality sub-type, and the higher risk of developing PTSD could be the consequence of both sharing the same genetic and/or pre-existing factors.

The following are some of the pre-existing factors that have been found to have possible associations with PTSD:

- Previous academic difficulties
- Family instability
- Abuse during childhood
- Increased willingness to serve

It is not clear how these pre-existing factors increase their risk of PTSD. It could be that it influences their perception of the traumatic incident. For example, an increased willingness to serve could result in more meaning being attached to the traumatic event. Previous academic difficulties could be deemed as failure and in a life of many failures there is nothing to fall back on during the incident of traumatic experience. It could be that these pre-existing factors rob them of their social fabric of support (e.g. family instability, abuse during childhood, etc) that can hold them together during the traumatic experience.

Some studies have shown that genetic factors pre-dispose the person to PTSD. PTSD have been found to be more highly correlated in monozygotic twins (born of the same embryo) than in dizygotic twins (born of different embryos).[8] Some people have criticized that these studies did not consider the possibility that monozygotic twins had higher correlation of shared non-combat experiences than dizygotic twins. The monozygotic twins could have had more shared experiences prior to the trauma that could have influenced the findings of higher correlation of PTSD.

Personality changes

Sherwood, Funari and Piekarski[9] examined 189 Vietnam veterans who had suffered chronic post traumatic problems for up to 20 years or more. The study hypothesized that their personality changes could be associated with their chronic disability. In fact, many forms of personality disorders have been associated with onset after traumatic events. Some associated disorders are as follows:

- *Schizoid personality disorder*—Detachment from social relationships and a restricted range of expression of emotions in interpersonal settings.

- Avoidant personality disorder–Social inhibition, feelings of inadequacy, and hypersensitivity to negative evaluation.

- Borderline personality disorder–Instability in interpersonal relationships, self-image, and affects, and marked impulsivity.

- Antisocial personality disorder–Disregard for, and violation of, the rights of others.

- Multiple personality disorder–Multiple distinct personalities that can include some of each of the other personalities.

It would appear that many personality disorders could be caused by exposure to trauma. Donna Williams describes in "Nobody Nowhere" her different "alters". She appeared to be suffering from multiple personality disorder that originated from childhood abuse. One of the "alters" was "Willy" who appeared antisocial. The other "alter" was "Caroline" who appeared to have some features of borderline, narcissistic and histrionic personalities. Gunilla Gerland who is autistic describes in "A Real Person–Life on the Outside" her dependence on others. It is not difficult to conceive that people suffering from the *autistic spectrum disorder* may become overly dependent on others and appear to have a dependant personality disorder.

My girlfriend too appears to be suffering from mild avoidant personality disorder. This personality disorder seems to originate from her perceptions of childhood trauma. In primary one, for the whole year, she felt traumatized by a particular teacher. This teacher often screamed and ranted at her for making minor mistakes. The more she cried, the more the teacher raised her voice at her. My girlfriend lived in fear throughout the year. Being a Buddhist then, every night at home she would pray to her idealized gods that her teacher would spare her the subsequent day. Subsequently she developed a social impairment where she became introverted and felt an inability to assimilate with her peers. Even though this experience is seemingly minor in pathological terms, it could have formed lasting impressions and permanent altercations in her mind that have had long-lasting effects. I have asked her to start writing a journal about her fears that she encountered during that period. I am of the opinion that the rationalization of her fears can in a psychotherapeutic manner, resolve her current difficulties. I believe also that if she truly loves God, God will gradually heal her.

Acute Stress Disorder

Acute stress disorder is distinguished from PTSD by the definition that it must occur and resolve within the 4–week period after the traumatic event. Effectively it is the same as PTSD except that it is less severe in that the period of symptomatology is shorter.

Adjustment Disorder

The essential feature of an adjustment disorder is a psychological response to an identifiable stressor or stressors that results in the development of clinically significant emotional or behavioural problems. The adjustment disorder is a "catch all" for those people who have apparently experienced some stressful event in their life and responded with a significant dysfunction, but where their response do not meet the criteria for *post traumatic stress disorder* and/or the stressor cannot be considered extreme in pathological terms.

Mood disorders

Depression has always been linked with major loss or bereavement. It could be the loss of a job or family member that results in depression. Depression could also be triggered by the person's pessimistic thoughts about his existence and future. Often, traumatic experiences can also result in depression as many traumatic experiences also involve loss. Many empirical studies have confirmed this. In one study of 146 friends of adolescent suicide victims, 29% developed depressive illnesses with a mean duration of eight months.[10] There have also been anecdotal reports of hypomania following trauma.

Anxiety disorders

The following are some of the anxiety disorders that can result from traumatic experience:

- Generalized anxiety disorder–Prolonged period of persistent and excessive anxiety and worry.

- Specific phobias–Significant anxiety provoked by exposure to a specific feared object (blood, water, insects) or situation (driving, flying, enclosed places, etc).

- Obsessive compulsive disorders–With obsessions such as thoughts, ideas, impulses or images (which cause marked anxiety or distress) and/ or compulsions such as hand washing, counting, etc (which serve to neutralize anxiety).

The onset of many cases of anxiety disorders have been found to occur after traumatic experiences.

Other disorders

Some other disorders have been observed to have onset following a traumatic experience, as follows:

- Somatoform disorders–Presence of physical symptoms that suggest a general medical condition and are not fully explained by a general medical condition, by the direct effects of a substance, or by another mental disorder.

- Substance use disorder–Abuse of substances such as alcohol, drugs, etc.

- Dissociative amnesia–Inability to recall important personal information, usually of a traumatic or stressful nature.

- Dissociative fugue–Sudden, unexpected travel away from home or one's customary place of work, accompanied by an inability to recall one's past and confusion about personal identity or the assumption of a new identity

- Physical illnesses–Increased rates of Graves' disease, thyroid disorders, cardiac disease, cancer and even death have been associated with trauma.

Genes and autism

In one British twin study[11] and a follow-up study[12] on the genetic links of *autism*, four main findings were crucial:

- The concordance rates for *autism* between monozygotic pairs (60%) and dizygotic pairs (5%) confirmed earlier findings on the strength of the genetic influence. Quantitative analysis indicated heritability in excess of 90%.

- The exceedingly low rate of concordance of dizygotic pairs compared with monozygotic pairs pointed to the likelihood of synergistic interaction among several genes. This means that more than one gene is responsible for *autism*. The falloff in rate from monozygotic and dizygotic twins, together with first-degree to second-degree relatives, was used to estimate the number of genes that likely were to be involved.[13] The findings effectively ruled out the possibility of just one gene, and suggested that three or four genes were most probable, but any number between 2 and 10 genes was a possibility (depending on the relative strength of effect of any one of these).

- Some 90% of monozygotic pairs were concordant for mixtures of social and cognitive deficits qualitatively similar to those found in traditional *autism*, but milder in degree.

- There was enormous clinical heterogeneity even when pairs shared exactly the same genes. Autistic individuals within monozygotic twin pairs were no more alike in IQ or symptomatology than were pairs of individuals selected at random from different twin pairs.

The findings support my earlier postulations as follows:

- Both the onset of PTSD and *autism* are influenced by genetic factors. This does not contradict the postulation that *autism* is also caused by trauma.

- More than one gene is responsible for *autism*. My hypothesis is that *autism* is caused by trauma: the trauma elicits a neurological response, which in turn triggers an endocrinological response. While trauma itself is an external factor, the perception of trauma is an internal factor. Hence in simplistic terms, one gene could be responsible for the perception of trauma. Another gene could be responsible for the neurological response and a third gene could be responsible for the endocrinological response. This is in line with the estimation of three of four responsible genes.

- In monozygotic twin pairs, the high concordance of social and cognitive deficits that may or may not be diagnosed as *autism*, indicates that *autism* lies on a continuous spectrum of differing severity where milder forms may not be diagnosed as *autism*.

- The enormous clinical heterogeneity found in monozygotic pairs indicates that the severity of *autism* and concurrent mental retardation do not depend on genetic factors but on other factors. This does not contradict the postulation that the symptomatology depends on age of onset and nature/extent of the trauma.

- The fact that monozygotic twins are not always concordant for *autism* indicates that non-genetic factors also play a part in the determination of *autism*. This does not contradict the postulation that *autism* is caused by trauma.

The 60% concordance rate for monozygotic pairs indicates high heritability. However this concordance rate may be overstated as monozygotic twins may have higher correlation of shared experiences than dizygotic twins. Shared experiences may mean higher concordance of risk of exposure to trauma or higher concordance of pre-existing factors that may pre-dispose the twins to perceive the event as traumatic. For example, the parent may abuse both the monozygotic twins because they look alike and abuse only one of the two dizygotic twins because their appearance is different.

The strong heritability for *autism* seems to indicate that the younger the age of onset of the disorder, the stronger the genetic influence. Genes play a more important role and the nature of the traumatic event a less important role at the delicate age. Genes may pre-dispose the infant to perceive minor stressful events as being traumatic. When the person is older, his perception of the traumatic event is less influenced by his genes but more a function of the actual event and his memory, identity, cognition, consciousness and perception. The susceptibility of the older person to the traumatic event is dependent more on the nature of the stressful event, and the pre-existing non-genetic factors that have defined the person prior to the event.

Magnification of trauma

From my own experience and the anecdotal experiences of others, it appears to me that trauma can be magnified by pre-conception. That is, if the traumatic experience can be related to a fearful memory, the response to the experience may be more significant. For example, if someone points a gun at your head and you have memories of many similar images that you have seen on TV and that these images have been associated with subsequent images of blood and gore, then this makes your perception of the experience even more traumatic. Hence, depictions of horror and violence in the media may be responsible for the observed upsurge of *pervasive development disorders, post traumatic stress disorders* and post traumatic illnesses in recent years.

Repetition can also magnify the severity of the effects of trauma. It has been observed that many rape victims suffer from chronic post traumatic symptomatologies. The act of rape is repetitive in nature. The initial entry would already have left an indelible mark on the consciousness. The second and subsequent entries would be even more traumatic because the relation of the subsequent entries to the fearful memory of the initial entry would already have been firmly established. Military personnel who see their comrades die in battle are also more likely to be traumatized as these memories add to their imagination when considering their own predicament.

Media, sex and rape

Studies have shown that increased exposure to sexual material in the media intensifies the sexual behaviour of adolescents. Without doubt, the media is also partly at fault for the increased sexual immorality in recent years.

Increased sexual material in the media can also increase the incidents of rape. When conceiving the act of rape, intrusive images of the "naked body" must be evident in the consciousness of the rapist. It is the pre-meditated conception of the gratification that brings about the act. How then is this conception formed? The media should take a fair share of the blame for its role in defining these images.

Sin and trauma

It appears to me that a world without "sin" would be a world with significantly less traumatic experiences.

What is sin? Sin is simply that which is unrighteous and in violation of conscience and divine law. I have included some excerpts from the Bible for us to better understand "sin":

"The acts of the sinful nature are obvious: sexual immorality, impurity and debauchery; idolatry and witchcraft; hatred, discord, jealousy, fits of rage, selfish ambition, dissensions, factions and envy; drunkenness, orgies, and the like. I warn you, as I did before, that those who live like this will not inherit the kingdom of God." (Galatians 5: 19–21)

"Put to death, therefore, whatever belongs to your earthly nature: sexual immorality, impurity, lust, evil desires and greed, which is idolatry. Because of these, the wrath of God is coming. You used to walk in these ways, in the life you once lived. But now you must rid yourself of all such things as these: anger, rage, malice, slander, and filthy language from your lips." (Colossians 3: 5–8)

"Among you there must not be any hint of sexual immorality, or of any kind of impurity, or of greed, because these are improper for God's holy people. Nor should there be obscenity, foolish talk or coarse joking." (Ephesians 5: 3–5)

"Rid yourself of all malice and all deceit, hypocrisy, envy, and slander of every kind. Like newborn babies, crave pure spiritual milk, so that by it you may grow up in your salvation, now that you have tasted that the Lord is good." (1 Peter 2: 1)

"He who does what is sinful is of the devil, because the devil has been sin-
ning from the beginning. The reason the Son of God appeared was to
destroy the devil's work." (1 John 3: 8)

To better understand sin, I have also included the antithesis to sin:

"But the fruit of the spirit is love, joy, peace, patience, kindness, goodness,
faithfulness, gentleness and self-control. Against such things there is no
law." (Galatians 5: 22–23)

"Therefore as God's chosen people, holy and dearly loved, clothe yourself
with compassion, kindness, humility, gentleness and patience. Bear with
each other and forgive whatever grievances you may have against one
another. Forgive as the lord forgave you. And over all these virtues put on
love, which binds them all together in perfect unity." (Colossians 3: 12–14)

"Finally, brothers, whatever is true, whatever is noble, whatever is right,
whatever is pure, whatever is lovely, whatever is admirable–if anything is
excellent or praiseworthy–think about such things." (Philippians 4: 8)

"The most important one,' answered Jesus, 'is this: "Hear, O Israel, the
Lord our God, the Lord is one. Love the Lord your God with all your
heart and with all your soul and with all your mind and with all your
strength." The second is this: "Love your neighbour as yourself." There is
no commandment greater than these'" (Mark 12: 29–31)

It is however impossible for man to overcome sin because by our nature, we
are sinful:

"I know that nothing good lives in me, that is, in my sinful nature. For I
have the desire to do what is good, but I cannot carry it out. For what I do
is not the good I want to do; no, the evil I do not want to do–this I keep
on doing. Now if I do what I do not want to do, it is no longer I who do
it, but it is sin living in me that does it. So I find this law at work: When I
want to do good, evil is right there with me. For in my inner being I
delight in God's law; but I see another law at work in the members of my
body, waging war against the law of my mind and making me a prisoner
of the law of sin at work within my members." (Romans 7: 18–23)

Only through the grace of God and Jesus Christ can we be redeemed from our sins and gain victory over "sin":

> "What the law was powerless to do in that it was weakened by the sinful nature, God did by sending his own Son in the likeness of sinful man to be a sin offering. And so he condemned sin in sinful man." (Romans 8: 3)

> "Those who belong to Christ Jesus have crucified the sinful nature with its passions and desires." (Galatians 5: 24)

> "Then Christ would have had to suffer many times since the creation of the world. But now he has appeared once for all at the end of the ages to do away with sin by the sacrifice of himself." (Hebrews 9: 26)

> "When you were dead in your sins and in the uncircumcision of your sinful nature, God made you alive with Christ. He forgave us all our sins, having cancelled the written code, with its regulations, that was against us and that stood opposed to us; he took it away, nailing it to the cross. And having disarmed the powers and authorities, he made a public spectacle of them, triumphing over them by the cross." (Colossians 2: 13–15)

> "God made him who had no sin to be sin for us, so that in him we might become the righteousness of God." (2 Corinthians 5: 21)

A possible hypothesis

Trauma can cause various mental illnesses. It can lead to serotogenic disturbances in the central nervous system that can result in mood and anxiety disorders. It can lead to serotogenic malfunction in the endocrine system that can result in the *autistic spectrum disorder*. Furthermore, it can disrupt the usually integrated functions of consciousness, memory, identity and perception, and lead to dissociation, somatoform disorders and personality disorders.

Serotogenic disturbances have been linked with both depression and anxiety disorders. Traumatic experience may sometimes cause regulatory dysfunction of serotonin production in the central nervous system. This book has also postulated that the *autistic spectrum disorder* results from serotogenic malfunction in the endocrine system. Until now however, little is known about the effect of trauma on the integrated functions of the mind.

Physical trauma can result in brain damage and scientists have noted that the brain may adapt to permanent impairment in one part of the brain by employing other parts of the brain to take over the same role. In the same way, psychological trauma may cause certain parts of the brain to become temporarily non-functional during the traumatic episode. This may be a protective bid to reject the consolidation of the painful experience into cognition and memory. During this period of non-function, other parts of the brain may relieve the afflicted area of its function and temporarily take on the same function. This may lead to subsequent conflicts and disruptions in consciousness, memory, identity and perception. Altered or multiple identities may originate, and traumatic memories may be forgotten. The newly incepted part of the brain may permanently take on its own definition. This definition may take the form of an identity (personality disorders) or physical expressions (somatoform disorders).

Psychotherapy appears to work by the remembrance of the traumatic event. Memories of the traumatic event may be found in both the traumatically deteriorated part of the brain and its unlikely substitute. Recollection of shared memories can provide a bridge between the afflicted area and its substitute, and this can lead to rationalization and integration of their functions. This may resolve any conflicts and lead to the healing of any prevailing fragmentation of the mind.

Important Points to Remember

- Trauma can result in normal response, *post traumatic stress disorders* and post traumatic illnesses;

- Post traumatic illnesses include mood, anxiety, personality, somatoform, substance use and dissociative disorders;

- There is evidence that the current boundaries that define the "stressors" for *post traumatic stress disorders* and post traumatic illnesses should be relinquished; the person's perception of the traumatic event determines his response to the "stressor" and not the nature of the event by itself; even pathologically minor events may be considered traumatic;

- Other than the traumatic event, the person's personality, experiences, genetic pre-disposition and most importantly his perception of the traumatic event also likely explain the development of *post traumatic stress disorders*;

- Both the onset of *post traumatic stress disorders* and *autism* are influenced by genetic factors;

- More than one gene is responsible for *autism*; best estimation is about three to four responsible genes;

- The *autistic spectrum* is a continuous spectrum where the severity of the symptomatologies is not mostly determined by genetic factors;

- Genetic factors seem to be more predominant for early onset of the disorder;

- Trauma can be magnified by pre-conception and repetition;

- A world without "sin" would be a world with significantly less traumatic experiences;

- Trauma can disrupt the usually integrated functions of consciousness, memory, identity and perception, and lead to dissociation, somatoform disorders and personality disorders;

- This disruption may occur as a result of confusions in brain functions in the face of trauma; and

- These confusions may be resolved by the rationalization of traumatic memories.

12

Confessions of Girlfriend

As Friends

We got to know each other through the freshman orientation camp in our University days. I was then in the second year and Irving, in his third year. We were both counsellors in the same orientation group. The first impression I had of him was that he is more reserved in nature and well...good looking. We seldom talked to each other but he left an impression on me. His reserved nature also made him out to be rather mysterious. After the camp, we continued to go out in a group.

As time passed, my interest in him grew and I felt chemistry between us. To me, chemistry was necessary in a relationship. From our common friends, I learnt that he also had some liking for me. I waited for him to make the first move but he did not. Later on, when my friends sounded him out, he said that he was not interested as he was not ready for a relationship. His reason being that he had some problem. None of us knew what his problems were.

I was curious and refused to give up so easily. I could not understand what could be so serious that one could not be in a relationship. I decided to make the first move because I strongly believed in having no regrets in life.

It took me a lot of courage to raise the topic with him. I remember we were having a group barbeque at the beach. I prayed for God's guidance as I was still deliberating over whether I should approach him. In our culture, it is unconventional for girls to profess their liking for guys. It was already late at night and Irving had not turned up for the barbeque. I thought that the outcome was by now obvious. However, Irving unexpectedly took a cab to join us after midnight. I took this as God's "go-ahead" signal. With renewed courage, I found an opportunity to tell him that I liked him and that the liking appeared mutual. Again, he said that he had problems and was not ready to enter into a relationship. He refused to divulge more and I was shattered. I needed good reasons.

I wanted to give up on him but believing that our feelings were mutual, it was hard for me to give up. I knew that he had some problems and I wanted so much to help him. On his birthday, I even made paper cranes for him and bought him presents, but he did not say much. I asked him again if he wanted to give our relationship a second thought, and received the same answer from him. All that I had managed to get out of him was that his problems were something physical yet psychological. I prayed hard for a miracle to happen. On 17 December 2000, I attended his baptism ceremony.

Things started to change. On the Christmas Eve not long after his baptism ceremony, he asked me to join him for a celebration with his friends. After that, things moved fast. We started to go out on frequent dates and became a couple. God had answered my prayers.

In a relationship

At the start of the relationship, he mentioned that he would change drastically as time passes. I took this only as a passing remark and did not give it much significance.

In the initial stages of the relationship, he needed lots of reassurances. He kept asking me if I regretted entering into the relationship, and if I did, I was to let him know. He asked the same question repeatedly a few times each day and I had to reassure him on each occasion.

We were both first-timers in the arena of love. I had this fixed mindset of what a relationship should be and certain expectations of how a boyfriend should act. He was however the complete opposite of most of my expectations. He is both passive and unromantic. On our first Valentine's Day together, I even had to outright tell him that I wanted flowers and how and where we were to celebrate. He did not like planning for such events as they meant little to him. When I suggested celebrating his birthday, his reply was that birthdays did not mean anything to him and a celebration was not necessary. He also showed no appreciation for the gifts (i.e. paper cranes, jigsaw puzzles, paper hearts) that I made for him. When my birthday came, once again I had to tell him what I wanted for my birthday and how we should go about celebrating. There were never any surprises for me. I chose my own presents and planned my own birthday celebrations. Almost everything was decided by me.

We have been together for nearly 4 years, and during this time, I have received flowers only twice from him. On both occasions, I requested for these flowers. When I asked him for flowers for the recent Valentine's Day, he remarked that he did not understand why women liked flowers and especially on Valentine's Day when they are so costly. Despite my request, he did not buy any flowers for me. Irving considers Valentine's Day as a commercialized event and a gimmick for companies to make money. Surprises are also superficial to him. I wanted to place some meaning on these occasions into his life but it was fruitless. He is too practical and logical. He is also unable to relate to what women want. Women are ruled more by emotions and men more by logic. However, he is an extreme case. When I tried to explain to him what a woman needs, he did not agree and could not understand. He always has a mind of his own and thinks that he is always right.

Women sometimes need to be showered with care and concern but there was little from him. I was down with a fever once, but it did not occur to him to look me up even when he was nearby in the vicinity. When I went for the lasik eye surgery, he did not even come to visit me. He did not even take the initiative to call me up to ask about the surgery. I had to phone him both before and after the surgery. He felt that lasik surgery was a cosmetic surgery that was being carried out because of my own vanity and that it was not necessary and totally frivolous. He also considered that there was nothing to be afraid about as the day surgery did not even require hospitalization. I explained to him that I felt uncomfortable wearing optical aids and that my contact lens always got torn and each time I had to fork out a few hundred dollars for the replacement. Despite this, he did not seem to understand and remained firm in his beliefs. I was very disappointed in his lacklustre attitude. All surgeries are risky and he should have at least phoned me.

Perhaps I demanded too much from him because of my idealistic image of a "boyfriend". On the other hand, because of his problem, he was a mediocre boyfriend. This led to many quarrels. Every time we quarrelled, he was very stubborn and seldom gave in to me. I felt insecure and our relationship worsened.

He also had "mood swings". He sometimes felt "high" and sometimes depressed. It was cyclical and I was like on a roller coaster ride with him. When he feels "high", he is very optimistic, talks a lot and sometimes without much thought. When he is depressed, he becomes very quiet and pessimistic. At some point in time, he became very uncertain of his thoughts and whether they truly defined him. Because of this uncertainty, I felt even more insecure.

He always attributes his actions to his after-effect. I was sceptical at first as he did not explain his problem to me clearly. I remember that when we just got attached, he told me that he needed another few months to solve his problem. However, months turned to years and I must admit that most of the time, I did not really believe that his therapy worked as he was very secretive about it.

Irving was also a very indecisive person. For example, when I asked him to decide on what to have for meals or which movies to watch, his answer would usually be "you decide". This really exasperated me.

We do not do what normal couples do. In a normal relationship, there are kissing and hugging but we seldom have any physical intimacy. Usually I have to request for it. He does not take the initiative and when I ask him for the reason, he attributes it to his after-effect and does not deem it as necessary. He does not like to hold hands, especially locking his fingers with mine. He feels really uncomfortable with it. Personally, I think that it is necessary to have physical intimacy in a relationship. Irving is also easily embarrassed when portraying physical intimacy in front of other people we know. Even holding hands in front of others is prohibited.

He also has memory impairment. If I mention something to him, he would forget about it very quickly. Often, I have to remind him to do certain things.

The change in him

I can see significant changes in him. In the past, he was more reserved when with people. Now, he is friendlier and much more cheerful. Our relationship has also improved. I can really see God's grace and work in his life. As I come to know more about the *autistic spectrum disorder*, I am able to empathize and understand more of what he went through during his 18 years of hardship. I strongly believe that he will be able to help many people with his book.

Afterword

About this book

This book may contain some inaccuracies for three reasons. Firstly, this book was written during both the heights of mania and the depths of depression. The inconsistencies in mood may have altered perception and reality. The second reason is that trauma causes fragmentation of memories. Discrete memories may be remembered but not their relationships. I have pieced together all my discrete memories in the most logical manner possible but there may still be some inaccuracies. Lastly, many mysteries are uncovered in this book. As I do not have all the pieces of this mysterious puzzle, I have filled up the gaps with both imagination and rationale.

A paradigm shift

The *autistic spectrum disorder* spans across various fields of medical science: psychiatry, endocrinology and neurology. The condition necessary for its trigger is psychological, the malfunction is endocrinological in nature and its effect is neurological:

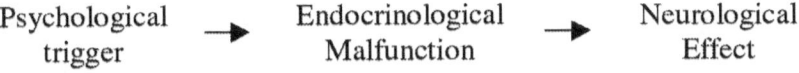

| Psychological trigger | → | Endocrinological Malfunction | → | Neurological Effect |

Thyroid disorder which was formally recognized as a mental illness prior to our understanding of its aetiology is also of a similar mechanism. After the mystery surrounding its aetiology was unravelled, it is no longer considered as a psychiatric illness.

It is perhaps time for us to change our understanding of psychiatric illnesses as being broadly psychological in nature. While some psychiatric illnesses may originate from a psychological trigger, the continuing disorder and its effect are likely due to chemical imbalances of an endocrinological and/or neurological nature. Other mental illnesses may not even be related to psychology and may originate directly from an endocrinological or neurological trigger. If this is proven true, most mental illnesses will no longer be considered as psychiatric illnesses but as physical disorders, not very much different from other physical diseases.

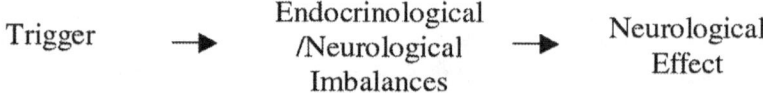

Two main neurotransmitters: Serotonin and Dopamine have been implicated in most mental illnesses. Perhaps most if not all mental illnesses are caused by imbalances in either one or both of these neurotransmission systems.

Current Thoughts

The removal of the serotogenic malfunction has brought about much calm and peace. The pace of my thoughts seems to have slowed to being manageable and is now very much aligned with my surroundings and life. My thoughts are now clearer, better organized and more integrative.

My visual sense of the surroundings is very much improved, with considerable enhancement in its clarity. This enhanced ability to sense my surroundings gives me a sense of peace. The sense of peace brings about a feeling very much similar to drinking a cup of water when I am thirsty. It is both refreshing and satisfying.

The improvement in my visual sense can be illustrated by the recent improvement in my soccer skills. I can now take sight of the goal mouth as I shoot at goal, be aware of my team-mates as I pass to them and keep my opponents in view as I dribble pass them. I previously played soccer with an obscure sense of the artefacts and the people around me. Now, my visual sense is no longer impaired and I am more aware of my surrounding artefacts and people and in general, the things that are happening around me.

I have also recently noticed that many actresses on TV apply lots of make-up on the screen. In the past even though I knew this for a fact, I found the actresses really pretty and thought that it was just their natural beauty. However now that I can better observe their make-up, they appear rather unnatural and very much painted.

Calmness also comes in part because of the reduced general and situational anxieties. I am no longer generally anxious. Neither do I get anxious easily even in tense situations.

My verbal communication has also improved. While my previous conversations with others had mostly been mono-syllabic and full of passivity, my conversations now consist of more content and creativity, and actually seeks to engage the other party.

Life is now more meaningful with the improved connection and better engagement. I no longer only partake in a restricted repertoire of activities. The improved engagement in life's activities results in more meaning being placed on them. The choice of activity that I want to partake in can now be decided by the meaning that is being placed on it.

In a sense, I have become more of a filial son, an understanding boyfriend, a chummy friend and an affable acquaintance. I am better able to empathize with people and show more care and concern. I can better understand their needs and intentions. This comes with an increased propensity to feel normal emotions. It is when one is able to feel normal emotions of love, happiness, hope and even sadness that one is able to empathize and reciprocate. The aberrant emotions of hypomania and depression are by now mostly extinguished.

The capacity for normal emotions, the verbal fluency, the calmness, the enhanced sensual connection and the attribution of meaning to life all add up to the enhancement of social connections. This can be illustrated by a recent occasion when I met some acquaintances while having breakfast alone at a coffee shop. Usually I would either try to avoid them or if not possible try to keep the conversations abrupt. My previous conversations with such acquaintances are usually designed to humour the other party. I would put on an act of being interested in the conversation even though I am raring to make my escape. This time round, I was actually interested in the conversation and in what the other party had to say. This was not an isolated incident and I find that nowadays during my conversations with other people, there is an actual feeling of engagement.

About the future

I am not certain whether I have sustained any permanent head damage (PHD) during the onslaught of the trauma and the vicissitudes of the physiotherapeutic after-effects. Initial indications suggest that there are no permanent disabling deficits. There may however be minor abnormalities but none of them are life-impairing, and are hardly noticeable.

In some ways, the *autistic spectrum disorder* has shaped me into who I am today. Despite my being cured, I have maintained some of the traits and personality that have been developed over the many years I was afflicted with the disorder. I have also retained some of the habits of old.

On a personal note, I greatly rejoice at being cured but I am aware that some people with the *autistic spectrum disorder* would prefer to remain autistic as their entire self has been defined by the disorder. These people may not perceive the *autistic spectrum disorder* as a disorder as they may have already become accustomed to life in this manner. This is particularly so for those for whom onset of the disorder occurred at a very young age. However, undeniably there are many others who still harbour the hope that they can one day be "normal". Remember that it is God that brings them this hope!

My past remains hazy and is like a dream that I have just woken up from. I have little to form a basis for consideration of my future.

When I completed the book, I was considering a few options:
- Find a job based on my Engineering degree.
- Find a job based on having passed the third level of Chartered Financial Analyst examinations.
- Find a job where I can dutifully serve God.
- Set up a small business.

- Write another book.
- Study psychiatry in the University.
- Study theology in the University.
- Possibly win the Nobel Prize. ☺

I am now working as an equities analyst. I am taking it one step at a time according to God's guidance. The first thing on my mind is to publish this book even if I have to self-publish using the vanity press. I have also set my sights on possibly writing another book titled "Agape".

When I quit my job to write this book, I was full of uncertainty. Uncertainty is more predominant while in the vicissitudes of the physiotherapeutic after-effects. During that time, God gave me His assurance that He would take care of my future with the following verse:

> "Look at the birds of the air; they do not sow or reap or store away in barns, and yet your heavenly Father feeds them......So do not worry, say-ing, 'What shall we eat?' or 'What shall we drink?' or 'What shall we wear?' For the pagans run after all these things, and your heavenly Father knows that you need them. But seek first his kingdom and his righteous-ness, and all these things will be given to you as well. Therefore do not worry about tomorrow, for tomorrow will worry about itself. Each day has enough trouble of its own." (Matthew 6: 26–34)

References

CHAPTER 3:
AUTISTIC SPECTRUM DISORDER

1. Heltzer, J.E., Robins, L.N., & McEvoy, L. (1987). Post-traumatic stress disorder in the general population. *New England Journal of Medicine*, 317(26), 1639–1634.

2. Breslau, N., Davis, G.C., & Andreski, P. (1991). Traumatic events and post traumatic stress disorder in an urban population of young adults. *Archives of General Psychiatry*, 48, 216–222.

3. Saxe, G., van der Kolk, B.A., Hall, K., Schwartz, J., Chinman, G., Hall, M.D., Lieberg, G., & Berkowitz, R. (1993). Dissociative disorders in psychiatric inpatients. *American Journal of Psychiatry*, 150(7), 1037–1042.

4. Friedman, M. J., Charney, D. S., & Deutch, A. Y. (1995). Neurobiological and clinical consequences of stress: From normal adaptation to post-traumatic stress disorder. *Hagerstown, MD, Lippincott-Raven.*

    van der Kolk, B. A., "The body keeps the score: Approaches to the psychobiology of posttraumatic stress disorder," In van der Kolk, B. A., Mac Farlane, A.C., & Weisaeth, L. (Eds.) (1996). Traumatic stress: The effects of overwhelming experience on mind, body and society. *NY, Guilford*, 214–241.

5. Southwick, S. M., Krystal, J. H., Morgan, C. A., Johnson, D., Nagy, L., Nicolaou, A., Henniger, G. R., & Charney, D. S. (1993). Abnormal

noradrenergic function in post traumatic stress disorder. *Archives of General Psychiatry*, 50: 266–274.

Charney, D. S., Deutsch, A. Y., Krystal, J. H., Southwick, S. M., & Davis, M. (1993). Psychobiologic mechanisms of post traumatic stress disorder. *Archives of General Psychiatry*, 50: 294–305.

DeBellis, M. D., & Putnam, F. W. (1994). The psychobiology of childhood maltreatment. *Child and Adolescent Psychiatric Clinics of North America*, 3, 663–667.

Yehuda, R., & MacFarlane, A. C. (1995). Conflict between current knowledge about posttraumatic stress disorder and its original conceptual basis. *American Journal of Psychiatry*, 152: 1705–1713

6. Bremner, J. D., Krystal, J. H, Southwick, S. M., & Charney, D. S. (1995). Functional neuroanatomical correlates of the effects of stress on memory. *Journal of Traumatic Stress*, 8 (1995): 527–554.

    Bremner, J. D., Randall, P., Scott, T. M., Bronen, R. A., Seibyl, J. P., Southwick, S. M., Delaney, R. C., McCarthy, G., Charney, D. S., & Innis, R. B. (1995). MRI-based measures of hippocampal volume in patients with posttraumatic stress disorder. *American Journal of Psychiatry*, 15: 973–981.

    Metzger, L. J., Orr S. P., Lasko, N. B., & Pitman, R. K. Reduced P3S in survivors of childhood sexual abuse with posttraumatic stress disorder. *Poster Presentation at the Annual Meeting of the International Society for Traumatic Stress Studies, San Francisco, CA, November 11, 1996.*

7. Bauman M., & Kemper T. Neuroanatomic observations of the brain in autism. *In the neurobiology of autism. Edited by Bauman M., Kemper T. Baltimore: Johns Hopkins University Pres; 1994.*

8. van der Ploerd, H. M., & Kleijin, W. C. (1989). Being held hostage in the Netherlands: A study of long-term aftereffects. *Journal of Traumatic Stress*, 2: 153–170.

9. Bettleheim, B. (1967). The empty fortress: Infantile autism and the birth of the self. *New York: The Free Press.*

10. Janet, P. (1889). L'Automatisme Psvcholoqique. Paris: Alcan.

11. Kardiner, A. (1941). The traumatic neuroses of war. *New York: Hoeber.*

12. van der Kolk, B. A., van der Hart, O., Burbridge, J. Approaches to the Treatment of PTSD.

13. Card, *Lives after Vietnam.*

14. Mary de Young. (1982). Self-injurious behaviour in incest victims: A research note. *Child Welfare,* 61: 577–584.

    Leibenluft, E., Gardner, D. L., & Cowdry, R. W. (1987). The inner experience of the borderline self-mutilator. *Journal of Personality Disorders,* 11: 317–324.

15. Kolb, L. C. (1989). Letter to the editor. *American Journal of Psychiatry,* 146: 811–812.

16. van der Kolk, B. A., & Fisler, R. (1995) Dissociation and the fragmentary nature of traumatic memories: review and experimental confirmation. *Journal of Traumatic Stress,* 8: 505–525.

17. Cardena, E. & Spiegel, D. (1993). Dissociative reactions to the Bay Area earthquake. *American Journal of Psychiatry,* 150: 474–478.

    Coopman, C., Classen, C., & Spiegel, D. (1994). Predictors of posttraumatic stress symptoms among survivors of the Oakland/Berkeley, California, firestorm. *American Journal of Psychiatry,* 151: 902–907.

18. Walker, E.A., Katon, W.J., Neraas, K., Jemelka, R.P., Massoth, D. (1992) Dissociation in women with chronic pelvic pain. *American Journal of Psychiatry,* 149: 534–537.

19. Saxe, G.N., Chinman, G., Berkowitz, R., Hall, K., Lieberg, G., Schwartz, J., van der Kolk, B.A. (1994). Somatization in patients with dissociative disorders. *American Journal of Psychiatry,* 151: 1329–1334.

20. McFarlane, A.C., Atchison M., Rafalowicz, E., & Papay, P. (1994) Physical symptoms in post traumatic stress disorder. *Journal Psychosomatic Res.,* 38: 715–726.

21. Foerster, A., Lewis, S. W., Owen, M.J., & Murray, R. M. (1991) Premorbid adjustment and personality in psychosis: Effects of sex and diagnosis. *British Journal of Psychiatry*, 158, 171–176

22. Done, J.D., Johnstone, E.C., Frith, C.D., Golding, J. & Shepherd, P. M. (1991) Complications of pregnancy and delivery in relation to psychosis in adult life: Data from the British perinatal mortality survey sample. *British Medical Journal*, 302, 1576–1580.

23. van Krevelen, D. Arn. (1963). On the relationship between the early infantile autism and autistic psychopathy. *Acta Paedopsychiatrica*, 30, 303–323.

    Gillberg, C. (1991). Clinical and neurobiological aspects of Asperger syndrome in six family studies. In U. Frith (Ed.), *Autism and Asperger syndrome* (pp 122–146). Cambridge: Cambridge University Press.

24. Wolff, S., Narayan, S., & Moyes, B. (1988). Personality characteristics of parents of autistic children: A controlled study. *Journal of Child Psychology and Psychiatry*, 29, 143–153.

    Narayan, S., Moyes, B., & Wolff, S. (1990). Family characteristics of autistic children: A further report. *Journal of Autism and Developmental Disorders*, 20, 523–535.

25. Nagy, J., Szatmari, P. (1986). A chart review of schizotypal personality disorders in children. *Journal of Autism and Developmental Disorders*, 16(3), 351–367.

26. Bailey, A., Le Couteur, A., Gottesman, I., Bolton, P., Simonoff, E., Yuzda, E., & Rutter, M. (1995) Autism as a strongly genetic disorder: Evidence from a British twin study. *Psychological Medicine*, 25, 63–77.

27. Folstein, S., & Santangelo, S. L. (1998),. Unpublished raw data.

CHAPTER 6:
THE SEROTONIN CONNECTION

1. Friedman, P. A., Kappelman, A. H., & Kaufman, S. (1972). Partial purification and characterization of tryptophan hydroxylase from rabbit hindbrain. *Journal Biol. Chem.*, 247(13): 4165–4173.

    Fernstrom, J. D., & Wurtman, R. J. (1971). Brain serotonin content: physiological dependence on plasma tryptophan levels. *Science.* 173(992): 149–152.

    Schaechter, J. D., & Wurtnam, R. J. (1989). Tryptophan availability modulates serotonin release from rat hypothalamic slices. *J Neurochem.* 53(6): 1925–1933.

    Sharp, T., Bramwell, S. R., & Grahame-Smith, D. G. (1992). Effect of acute administration of L-tryptophan on the release of 5-HT in rat hippocampus in relation to serotogenic neuronal activity: An in vivo microdialysis study. *Life Sciences*, 50(17): 1215–1223.

2. Neumeister, A. (2003). Tryptophan depletion, serotonin, and depression: Where do we stand? *Psychopharmacology Bulletin*, 37(4): 99–115.

3. Linnoila, V. M., & Virkkunen, M. (1992). Aggression, suicidality, and serotonin. *J. Clin. Psychiatry*, 53 (Suppl.): 46–51

4. Lion, J. R. (1995). Aggression. *In Harold I. Kaplan and Benjamin J. Sadock, eds., Comprehensive Textbook of Psychiatry, vol. 1 (Baltimore, Md.: Williams & Wilkins).*, 310–317.

5. Riedel, W. J., Klaassen, T., Deutz, N. E., van Someren, A., & van Praag, H. M. (1999). Tryptophan depletion in normal volunteers produces selective impairment in memory consolidation. *Psychopharmacol. (Berl).*, 141(4): 362–369.

    Schmitt, J. A., Jorissen, B. L., Sobczak, S., van Boxtel, M. P., Hogervorst, E., Deutz, N. E., & Riedel, W. J. (2000). Tryptophan depletion impairs memory consolidation but improves focused attention in healthy young volunteers. *J Psychopharmacol.* 14(1): 21–29.

6.   Schain, R. J., & Freedman D. X. (1961). Studies on 5-hydroxyindole metabolism in autistic and other mentally retarded children. *J Pediatrics*, 58: 315–320.

7.   Anderson, G. M., Freedman, D. X., Cohen, D. J., Volkmar, F. R., Hoder, E. L., McPhedran, P., Minderaa, R. B., Hansen, C. R., & Young, J. G. (1987). Whole blood serotonin in autistic and normal subjects. *J. Child Psychol. Psychiat.*, 28: 885–900.

Cook, E. H. (1990). Autism: Review of neurochemical investigation. *Synapse 1990*, 6: 292–308.

8.   McDougle, C. J., et al. (1993). Acute tryptophan depletion in autistic disorder: A controlled case study. *Biol. Psychiatry*, 33: 547–550.

9.   Mehlinger, R., Sheftner, W. A., & Poznanski, E. (1990). Fluoxetine and autism. *J. Am. Acad. Child Adolesc. Psychiatry*, 29: 985.

McDougle, C. J., Price, L. H., & Goodman, W. K. (1990). Fluvoxamine treatment of coincident autistic disorder and obsessive compulsive disorder: A case report. *J. Aut. Develop. Disord.*, 20: 537–543.

Todd, R. D. (1991). Fluoxetine in autism. *Am. J. Psychiatry*, 148: 1089.

Cook, E., Rowlett, R., Jaselskis, C., & Leventhal, B. (1992). Fluoxetine treatment of patients with autism and mental retardation. *J. Am. Acad. Child Adolesc. Psychiatry*, 31: 739–745.

Gordon, C., State, R., Nelson, J., Hamburger, S., & Rapoport, J. (1993). A double-blind comparison of clomipramine, desipramine, and placebo in the treatment of autistic disorder. *Arch . Gen. Psychiatry*, 50: 441–447.

10. Rimland, B. (1988). Controversies in the treatment of autistic children: Vitamin and drug therapy. *J. Child Neurol.*, 3 (Suppl.): S68–72.

11. Pfeiffer, S. I., et al. (1995). Efficacy of vitamin B6 and magnesium in the treatment of autism: A methodology review and summary of outcomes. *J. Autism & Devel. Disorders*, 25: 481–493.

12. McDougle, C., Naylor, S., Cohen, D., Aghajanian, G., Heninger, G., & Price, L. (1996). Effects of tryptophan depletion in drug-free adults with autism. *Arch. Gen Psychiatry*.

13. Jacobs, B. L. (1991). Serotonin and behavior: Emphasis on motor control. *J. Clin. Psychiatry*, 52 (Suppl.): 17–23.

14. Valzelli, L. (1982). Serotogenic inhibitory control of experimental aggression. *Psychopharmacological Research Communications*, 12: 1–13.

15. Nagy, L. M., Morgan, C. A., Southwick, S. M., & Charney, D. S. (1993). Open prospective trial of fluoxetine for post traumatic stress disorder. *Journal of Clinical Psychopharmacology*, 13: 107–114.

16. van der Kolk, B. A., Dreyfuss, D., Berkowitz, R., Saxe, G., & Michaels, M. (1994). Fluoxetine in post traumatic stress. *Journal of clinical psychiatry.*

17. Bauman, M, & Kemper, T. (1994). Neuroanatomic observations of the brain in autism. In the Neurobiology of Autism. Edited by Bauman M, Kemper T. Baltimore: Johns Hopkins University Pres; 1994.

18. D' Eufemia, P., Finocchiaro, R., Celli, M., Viozzi, L., Monteleone, D., & Giardini, O. (1995) Low serum tryptophan to large neutral amino acids ratio in idiopathic infantile autism. *Biomedicine and Pharmacotherapy*, 49: 288–292.

CHAPTER 8:
PARALLELS WITH HYPERTHYROIDISM

1. Victoroff, V. M., Mantel, S. J., & Bailetti, A., et al. (1979). Physical examinations in psychiatric practice. *Ohio Hospital Commission of Psychiatry*, 30: 536–540.

2. Kathol, R. G., & Delahunt, J. W. (1986). The relationship of anxiety and depression to symptoms of hyperthyroidism using operational criteria. *General Hospital Psychiatry*, 8: 23–28.

3. Graves, R. J. (1835). Newly observed affection of the thyroid gland in females. *London Medical Surgical Journal*, 7, part 2: 516.

4. Collections from the unpublished writings of the late C. H. Parry, London, Underwoods, 1825.

5. Levey, J. K., Bell, K. E., & Lachar, B. L., et al. "Psychoneuroimmunol-ogy," in Neuroimmunology for the Clinician, edited by Loren A. Rolak and Yadollah Harati, 35–55 (Newton, Mass: Butterworth-Heinemann, 1997).

6. Howland, R. H. (1993) Thyroid dysfunction in refractory depression: Implications for pathophysiology and treatment. *Journal of Clinical Psychiatry*, 54, no. 2: 47–54.

7. Bernal, J. & Nunez, J. (1995). Thyroid hormones and brain development. *European Journal of Endocrinology*, 133: 390–398.

CHAPTER 11:
DIALECTIC OF TRAUMA

1. Breslau, N., & Davis, G. C. (1987). Posttraumatic stress disorder: The etiologic specificity of wartime stressors. 139th Annual Meeting of the American Psychiatric Association, 1986, Washington DC. *American Journal of Psychiatry*, 144, 5: 578–583.

2. Scott, M. J., & Stradling, S. G. (1994). Post-traumatic stress disorder without the trauma. *British Journal of Clinical Psychology*, 33, 1: 71–74.

3. Foy, D. W., Resnick, H. S., Sipprelle, R. C., & Carroll, E. M. (1987). Premilitary, military, and postmilitary factors in the development of combat-related posttraumatic stress disorder, *Behavior Therapist*, 10, 1: 3–9.

4. Foy, D. W., & Card, J. J. (1987). Combat-related post-traumatic stress disorder etiology: Replicated findings in a national sample of Vietnam-era men. *Journal of Clinical Psychology*, 43, 1: 28–31.

5. Fontana, A., & Rosenheck, R. (1993). A causal model of the etiology of war-related PTSD. *Journal of Traumatic Stress*, 6, 4: 475–500.

6. Holloway, H. C., & Ursano, R. J. (1984). The Vietnam veteran: Memory, social context, and metaphor. *Psychiatry*, 47, 2: 103–8.

7. Davidson, J., Kudler, H,. & Smith, R. (1987). Personality in chronic post-traumatic stress disorder: A study of the Eysenck inventory. *Journal of Anxiety Disorders*, 1, 4: 295–300.

8. True, W. R., Rice, J., Eisen, S. A., Heath, A. C., Goldberg, J., Lyons, M. J., & Nowak, J. (1993). A twin study of genetic and environmental contributions to liability for posttraumatic stress symptoms. *Archives of General Psychiatry*, 50, 4: 257–264.

9. Sherwood, R. J., Funari, D. J., & Piekarski, A. M. (1990). Adapted character styles of Vietnam veterans with posttraumatic stress disorder. *Psychological Reports*, 66, 2: 623–631.

10. Brent, D. A., Perper, J. A., Moritz, G., Liotus, L., Schweers, J., & Canobbio, R. (1994). Major depression or uncomplicated bereavement? A follow up of youth exposed to suicide. *Journal of the American Academy of Child and Adolescent Psychiatry*, 33, 2: 231–240.

11. Bailey, A., Le Couteur, A., Gottesman, I., Bolton, P., Simonoff, E., Yuzda, F. Y., & Rutter, M. (1995). Autism as a strongly genetic disorder: Evidence from a British twin study. *Psychological Medicine*, 25: 63–77.

12. Le Couteur, A., Bailey A. J., Goode, S., Pickles, A., Robertson, S., Gottesman, I. & Rutter, M. (1996). A broader phenotype of autism: The clinical spectrum in twins. *Journal of Child Psychology and Psychiatry*, 37: 785–801.

13. Pickles, A., Bolton, P., MacDonald, H., Bailey, A., Le Couteur, A., Sim, L., & Rutter, M. (1995). Latent class analysis of recurrence risk for complex phenotypes with selection and measurement error: A twin and family history study of autism. *American Journal of Human Genetics*, 57: 717–726.

Books

1. American Psychiatric Association. Diagnostic and Statistical Manual of Mental Disorders, Fourth Edition, Text Revision. Washington, DC, American Psychiatric Association, 2000.

2. Attwood, T. Asperger's Syndrome. London: Jessica Kingsley Publishers, 2000.

3. Edited by Klin, A., Volkmar F. R., & Sparrow, S. S. Asperger Syndrome. New York: The Guilford Press, 2000.

4. Waterhouse, S. A Positive Approach to Autism. London: Jessica Kingsley Publishers, 2000.

5. Gerland, G. A Real Person: Life on the outside. London: Souvenir Press, 1997.

6. Williams, D. Nobody Nowhere: The Extraordinary Autobiography of an Autistic. New York: Avon Books, 1992.

7. Baumel, S. Serotonin: How to Naturally Harness the Power behind Prozac and Phen/Fen. New Canaan, Connecticut, Keats Publishing, 1997.

8. Longstaff, A. Neuroscience. London: BIOS Scientific Publishers, 2000.

9. Atlas of Anatomy. Florence, Giunti Editorial Group. Translated by TAJ Books.

10. Arem, R. M.D. The Thyroid Solution. New York: Random House, 1999.

11. Herman, J. M.D. Trauma and Recovery. New York: Basic Books, 1997.

12. O'Brien, S. Traumatic Events and Mental Health. Cambridge, United Kingdom: Cambridge University Press, 1998.

13. McMahon, G. Coping with Life's Traumas. Dublin: Gill & Macmillan Ltd, 2000.

14. Park, C. C. Exiting Nirvana: A Daughter's Life with Autism. U.S.A.: Little, Brown and Company.

15. Grandin, T. Thinking in Pictures. New York: Random House, 1995.

978-0-595-38348-1
0-595-38348-3